N E T W O R K +
Lab Manual
for Guide to Networks

Todd Meadors

COURSE
TECHNOLOGY

Thomson Learning™

ONE MAIN STREET, CAMBRIDGE, MA 02142

Australia • Canada • Denmark • Japan • Mexico • New Zealand • Philippines
Puerto Rico • Singapore • South Africa • Spain • United Kingdom • United States

Network+ Lab Manual for Guide to Networks is published by Course Technology.

Associate Publisher	Kristen Duerr
Senior Acquisitions Editor	Stephen Solomon
Product Manager	David George
Production Editor	Megan Cap-Renzi
Developmental Editor	Ann Shaffer
Quality Assurance Manager	John Bosco
Associate Product Manager	Laura Hildebrand
Marketing Manager	Susan Ogar
Text Designer	GEX Inc.
Composition House	GEX Inc.
Cover Designer	Efrat Reis

Disclaimer

Course Technology reserves the right to revise this publication and make changes from time to time in its content without notice.

The Web addresses in this book are subject to change from time to time as necessary without notice.

For more information, contact Course Technology, One Main Street, Cambridge, MA 02142; or find us on the World Wide Web at *www.course.com*.

For permission to use material from this text or product, contact us by

- Web: *www.thomsonrights.com*
- Phone: 1-800-730-2214
- Fax: 1-800-730-2215

ISBN 0-619-01521-7

Printed in Canada

3 4 5 WC 04 03 02 01 00

TABLE OF CONTENTS

INTRODUCTION

The goal of this book is to give you insight into the networking field and to help prepare you for the Network+ exam. This book is suitable for use in a beginning or intermediate networking course.

As a prerequisite, you should have at least one year of computer experience. Passing the A+ certification exam would suffice in lieu of this experience. This book is best used when accompanied by the Course Technology textbook *Network+ Guide to Networks* or another introduction to networking textbook.

FEATURES

In order to ensure a successful experience for both instructors and students, this book includes the following features:

- **Objectives:** Every lab has a list of learning objectives.
- **Materials Required:** This lists all of the materials required for the lab.
- **Activity Sections:** The labs are broken down into manageable sections, including **Step-by-step instructions**.
- **Review Questions:** Questions, where appropriate, are included to make sure students are meeting the objectives of the lab activity.

ACKNOWLEDGEMENTS

I'd like to thank the people at Course Technology for their help. In particular, thanks to Stephen Solomon for giving me the opportunity to write this book. Thanks also to Dave George and Ann Shaffer for guidance throughout the writing process. I'm also grateful to Megan Cap-Renzi for shepherding the manuscript through the production process, and to John Bosco and the Quality Assurance staff for helping to ensure the accuracy of every step.

This book is dedicated to my family: Micki, Zac, and Jessie.

AN INTRODUCTION TO NETWORKING

Labs included in this chapter

➤ Lab 1.1 Understanding Elements of a Network

➤ Lab 1.2 Understanding How Networks Are Used

➤ Lab 1.3 Creating a Free Internet E-mail Account

➤ Lab 1.4 Searching for Networking Jobs

➤ Lab 1.5 Giving an Oral Presentation on the Networking Industry

➤ Lab 1.6 Using an Internet Encyclopedia

THomas Taylor

LAB 1.1 UNDERSTANDING ELEMENTS OF A NETWORK

Objectives

The goal of this lab is to allow you to see some real-life examples of basic networking concepts. In order to complete this lab, you will be required to visit a local business, school, church, or another organization and identify various networking components at that site. After visiting the site, you will be able to:

➤ Identify various network topologies

➤ Identify a network's servers, workstations, and printers

➤ Identify a network's network operating systems

➤ Identify a protocol used by the network

Materials Required

This lab will require the following:

➤ Someone willing to give you a tour of a network at a business, school, church, or another site

➤ Pencil and paper

ACTIVITY

1. Contact a business, school, church, or another organization and politely ask to interview the person in charge of their network. Explain that your purpose is purely educational and that you desire to learn more about networking. Also, explain that you will need to take notes.

2. Record the name of the organization: _____
   Brah Skate & Bowl .

3. Make the visit and observe the network. Remember to ask for details about the network's topology, hardware, operating system, and protocols.

4. On a separate piece of paper, draw the site's network topology, using boxes to represent the components such as computers and printers. Draw lines to connect the components.

5. On your diagram, label servers with the letter "S," workstations with the letter "W," and printer with the letter "P." If you are unsure about a network component, label the box with the letter "O" for "other."

6. Record the network operating system (NOS) type (or types) and version:
   Windows NT 4.0 .

7. Record the type of network interface cards (NICs): _____ .

1

8. Record the network's protocols: _____

9. Thank the person you interviewed.

10. Follow up with a letter of thanks.

Review questions

1. The term network topology is used to refer to a LAN's layout.
   T __✓__ F _____

2. A protocol is a device that allows a computer to connect to the network.
   T _____ F __✓__

3. Peer-to-peer networks always share centralized resources.
   T __✓__ F _____

4. The client/server architecture is used to describe two to three computers that are connected with no central file server.
   T _____ F __✓__

5. All computers use the same protocol.
   T _____ F __✓__

6. Define the term node. _Any Computer connected to a network_

7. Define the term address. _a number that uniquely identifies each workstation and device of network._

8. Which of the following are examples of network operating systems? Circle all that apply.
   a. NetWare
   b. UNIX
   c. DOS
   d. Windows NT

LAB NOTES

It is a good idea to keep the name of the contact from the organization you visit. It may just lead to a network job there someday.

LAB 1.2 UNDERSTANDING HOW NETWORKS ARE USED

Objectives

The goal of this lab is to help you learn more about how network servers are used in the real world. In order to complete this lab, you will be required to visit a site different from the one you visited in Lab 1-1. After visiting the site, you will be able to:

➤ Identify various types of network services used by an organization

Materials Required

This lab requires the following:

➤ Someone willing to give you a tour of a network at a business, school, church, or another site. The network should include at least one server

➤ Pencil and paper

ACTIVITY

1. Contact the person at the site. As in Lab 1-1, explain that your purpose is educational and that you will be taking notes about the network.

2. Make the visit and observe the network. Ask for descriptions of the network's file and print services, communications services, mail services, Internet services, and management services.

3. Record the names of the servers using File and Print Services:
   Cm Server

4. Record the names of the servers using Communication Services:
   Cm Server

5. Record the names of the servers using Mail Services:
   -NA-

6. Record the names of the servers using Internet Services:
   -NA-

7. Record the names of the servers using Management Services:

8. Thank the person you interviewed.

9. Follow up with a letter of thanks

Review Questions

1. A communications server allows remote connections through use of modems.
   T _____ F _____

1

2. Organizations never need to be concerned with backing up critical data of a file server.

   T __✔__ F _____

3. Using Print Services to share printers across a network saves money.

   T __✔__ F _____

4. If a firm uses a dedicated server to share a word-processing application, it is considered an Internet server.

   T __✔__ F _____

5. Internet services include Web servers and browsers, and file transfer capabilities.

   T __✔__ F _____

6. What would happen to the performance of a single server if it suddenly began to run all of the network services mentioned in this lab?

   The performance would slow down the server and take up memory.

   _____

7. Discuss the importance of server security. *Safeguards your internet Communications by requesting authentication for access*

   _____

8. Which of the following services would be considered Management Services? Circle all that apply.

   a. Load balancing
   b. Security
   c. Licensing
   d. Printing

LAB 1.3 CREATING A FREE INTERNET E-MAIL ACCOUNT

Objectives

In order to complete this lab, you will need access to the Internet. You can visit a local library if you have no other Internet access. After completing this lab, you will be able to:

➤ Create a free Internet e-mail account, allowing you to send and receive e-mail messages

Materials Required

This lab requires the following:

➤ A computer with access to the Internet

ACTIVITY

1. Start an Internet browser such as Microsoft Explorer or Netscape Navigator.

2. Go to **http://www.yahoo.com**. The Yahoo home page appears on your screen.

3. Click the **Check Email** icon. The Yahoo Mail screen appears.

4. Under the section titled "I'm a New User," click **Sign me up!**.

5. Read the agreement, and click the **I Accept** button. The **Sign up Now** screen appears.

6. Decide upon a Yahoo e-mail ID and enter it in the **Yahoo ID** text box.

7. Fill in the required screen information and then click the **Submit this Form** button. If any of the required information is not filled in or if the e-mail ID is currently being used, you will be prompted to correct the information and submit again. If the request is successful, you will see the **Yahoo Mail** screen.

8. At the top of the **Yahoo Mail** screen, identify your e-mail ID in the **Welcome** message. It should be the name you entered previously for your e-mail ID, followed by the text @yahoo.com. For example, if you entered Mike_Brown, Mike_Brown@yahoo.com would be your Yahoo e-mail ID.

9. Record your e-mail ID: _ebay3095 @ yahoo, com_ .

10. You can now use your Yahoo e-mail ID to send and receive e-mail from any location in the world; and unlike an e-mail account at an Internet service provider, it is free.

11. Exit Yahoo mail and the Web browser.

Review Questions

1. In order to send e-mail over the Internet, you must have access to an organization that is connected to the Internet.
   T ____✔____ F _____

2. You can use e-mail to send a message to a prospective employer.
   T ____✔____ F _____

3. With your e-mail ID, you can read your e-mail from any location in the world that has Internet access.
   T ____✔____ F _____

4. The most commonly used service in a network is e-mail.
   T ____✔____ F _____

5. Mail services can run on different kinds of network operating systems.
   T ____✔____ F _____

6. Discuss the advantages of placing your e-mail ID on your resume.

The advantages of placing your email ID on resume is _____

_____

_____

LAB 1.4 SEARCH FOR NETWORKING JOBS

Objectives

The goal of this lab is to help you learn more about searching for networking jobs over the Internet. In order to complete this lab, you will need access to the Internet. After completing this lab, you will be able to:

➤ Use the Internet to search for a job

Materials Required

This lab requires the following:

➤ A computer with access to the Internet

ACTIVITY

1. Start an Internet browser such as Microsoft Explorer or Netscape Navigator.

2. Go to **http://www.hotjobs.com**. The hotjobs.com home page appears.

3. In the Quick Search text box, enter **Network**, and then click the **Find me a Job!** button. A list of jobs appear on your screen.

4. Record the number of jobs that were returned: ___*1000*___.

5. Click the first job title in the list.

6. Record the job title: ___*Voice Technician*___

7. Scroll down and notice that you can cut and paste your resume into the form and apply for the job online.

8. Exit hotjobs.com and the Web browser.

Review Questions

1. Besides job seeking, describe other uses of the Internet.

Information, weather, Games, e-mail, How-to, Shop, sell, advertises _____

_____

2. Discuss the benefits of becoming a networking certified professional.

Better Salary, Greater Opportunities Professional respect, Access to better support _____

_____

3. Discuss methods of job searching other than use of the Internet.

Newspaper, Career Center, Career fairs

_____

_____

LAB 1.5 GIVING AN ORAL PRESENTATION ON THE NETWORKING INDUSTRY

Objectives

The goal of this lab is to allow you to share information on networking, just as you would when working as a networking engineer. In this lab, you will give an oral presentation to a group of two to three people based on your findings in Lab 1.1. After completing this lab, you will be able to:

- Give an oral presentation to a group

Materials Required

This lab requires the following:

- Completion of Lab 1.1

- An audience of at least three people

ACTIVITY

1. Identify the major points from your interview based on the items you recorded in Lab 1.1.

2. Record the major points: _____

_____

_____

_____.

3. Practice your presentation.

4. Give the presentation to a group of at least three other people.

5. Answer any questions from members in the group.

6. Identify one of the questions from the group.

7. Record the question: _____

_____.

8. Record the answer you gave: _____

_____.

9. Summarize the key points to the group.

Review Questions

1. What should you do if you are asked a question during a meeting with other engineers that you do not know the answer to?
   Tell the truth, that you don't know but you like to know more about it.

2. Discuss how teamwork skills are necessary in the networking field.
   teamwork skills are needed in this field because everybody have a job to do in order to connect computers together. You have to depend on others as you do your job.

3. Discuss how making an oral presentation will assist you on the job.
   Oral presentation will assist you on the job by letting other know that you can work well with a crowd and do a speech in front of people.

LAB 1.6 USING AN INTERNET ENCYCLOPEDIA

Objectives

The goal of this lab is to teach you how to research networking topics on the Internet. In this lab, you will use an Internet encyclopedia to research the definitions of networking terms. After completing this lab, you will be able to:

- Use the Internet to research networking terms

ACTIVITY

1. Start an Internet browser such as Microsoft Explorer or Netscape Navigator.

2. Go to **http://www.webopedia.com**. The Webopedia home page appears.

3. In the Search: dialog box, type **client** and click the **Go!** button. The Webopedia screen displays the definition.

4. In your own words, define the term client. *Client is a computer that relies on another computer for information.*

5. In the Search: dialog box, type **NIC** and then click the **Go!** button. The Webopedia screen displays the definition.

6. In your own words, define the term NIC. *a card that is put into your computer so you can be connected to the network.*

7. On the definition screen, locate the Related Terms section.

8. What is the first related term? _AUI_

9. Exit Webopedia and close your Internet browser.

Review Questions

In this section, you will use the Internet encyclopedia to define networking terms. Write them using your own words.

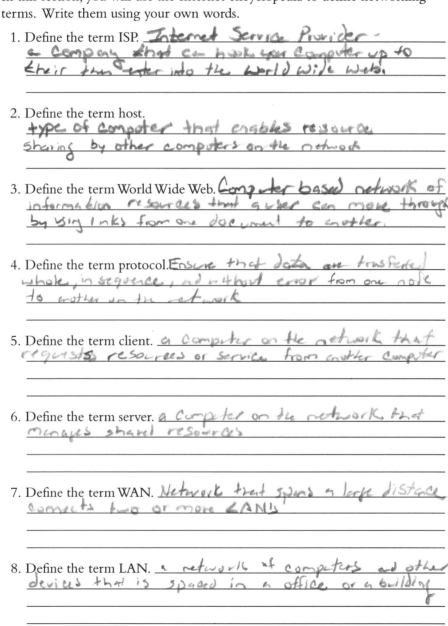

1. Define the term ISP. _Internet Service Provider - a company that can hook your computer up to their then enter into the world wide web._

2. Define the term host. _type of computer that enables resource sharing by other computers on the network_

3. Define the term World Wide Web. _Computer based network of information resources that a user can move through by using links from one document to another._

4. Define the term protocol. _Ensure that data are transferred whole, in sequence, and without error from one node to another on the network_

5. Define the term client. _a computer on the network that requests resources or service from another computer_

6. Define the term server. _a computer on the network that manages shared resources_

7. Define the term WAN. _Network that spans a large distance connects two or more LANs_

8. Define the term LAN. _a network of computers and other devices that is spaced in a office or a building_

NETWORKING STANDARDS AND THE OSI MODEL

LAB 2.1 NETWORKING STANDARDS ORGANIZATION

Objectives

The goal of this lab is to increase your awareness of the organizations that manage networking standards. In this lab, you will view the Web sites of two organizations that deal in networking standards. After completing this lab, you will be able to:

➤ Understand the purpose of networking standards organizations

Materials Required

This lab will require the following:

➤ An Internet connection

➤ Pencil and paper

ACTIVITY

1. Start an Internet browser such as Microsoft Explorer or Netscape Navigator.

2. Go to **http://www.ansi.org**. The ANSI home page appears.

3. Click the **About ANSI** link. The About ANSI page appears.

4. Read the information about this organization, and click the **Next** link to proceed to the next page.

5. Review the complete explanation of the purpose of ANSI. Use the right and left arrow buttons at the bottom of the pages to navigate among the About ANSI pages.

6. Write a summary of the purpose of ANSI. _____
   _____
   _____
   _____
   _____

7. Go to **http://www.iso.ch**. The ISO home page appears on your screen.

8. Click the **About ISO** link. The About ISO page appears.

9. Click the **Introduction to ISO** link. The Introduction to ISO page appears with several hyperlinks on the left-hand side of the screen.

10. Click the **What are standards?** link. The What are standards page appears. Scroll down to see the information that is referenced in the hyperlinks on the Introduction to ISO screen.

11. Read the information about this organization and write a summary of its purpose. _____

_____
_____
_____
_____

12. Exit the Web site and the Web browser.

Review Questions

1. What standards organization represents the United States in setting international standards? Circle the best answer.
   a. ANSI
   b. ISO
   c. ITU
   d. CCITT

2. What standards organization promotes development and education in the electrical engineering and computer science fields?
   a. ISO
   b. ANSI
   c. IEEE
   d. ITU

3. ISO's standards only affect the United States.
   T _____ F _____

4. Define the purpose of the International Telecommunications Union (ITU).

_____
_____
_____

5. Define the purpose of the Electronics Industry Alliance (EIA).

_____
_____
_____

6. Give an example that illustrates the importance of standards.

_____
_____
_____

LAB 2.2 THE OSI MODEL

Objectives

The goal of this lab is to help you learn more about the OSI model. After completing this lab, you will be able to:

➤ Identify the function of the layers of the OSI model

Materials Required

This lab will require the following:

➤ Pencil and paper

ACTIVITY

1. Read the following scenario: A secret agent must write a three-page letter to another secret agent in a small town 25 miles outside of Paris, France. Each page of the letter will be mailed separately because of the highly sensitive nature of the material. In order for the recipient to understand the entire letter, the recipient must have all three pages. Each word will be encrypted by the sending agent and again decrypted by the receiving agent. The sending agent will send the letter through the regular mail service but will use return receipt to guarantee delivery. The letter will be first sent to Paris and then forwarded to the small town.

2. Compare the parts of the addressed and stamped letter to a data frame.

   _____

   _____

3. List the layers of the OSI model and briefly state the function of each:

   _____

   _____

4. Compare the letter's journey through the postal system to the progress of a packet of data through the layers of the OSI model.

   Physical _____

   _____

   Data Link _____

   _____

   Network _____

   _____

   Transport _____

   _____

Session _____

Presentation _____

2

Application _____

Review Questions

1. The Presentation layer manages encryption and decryption.

   T _____ F _____

2. The Transport layer handles sequencing of packets.

   T _____ F _____

3. The Network layer is responsible for routing data from one network segment to another.

   T _____ F _____

4. Which layer of the OSI model deals with cable specifications?

   a. Application

   b. Presentation

   c. Physical

   d. Network

5. Which layer is responsible for reliable end-to-end communication?

   a. Application

   b. Session

   c. Presentation

   d. Physical

6. Which layer encrypts and decrypts data?

   a. Network

   b. Physical

   c. Presentation

   d. Data Link

7. Which layer divides data into frames?

   a. Data Link

   b. Presentation

   c. Application

   d. Network

8. Discuss the parts of a data frame. _____
_____
_____
_____

LAB 2.3 FRAME SPECIFICATIONS

Objectives

The goal of this lab is to help you learn more about Ethernet and Token Ring frame specifications. After completing this lab, you will be able to:

➤ Identify an Ethernet frame

➤ Identify a Token Ring frame

➤ Identify the elements common to both frames

Materials Required

This lab will require the following:

➤ Pencil and paper

ACTIVITY

1. Draw a picture of an Ethernet frame. Label the components of the frame.

2. Draw a picture of a Token Ring frame. Label the components of the frame.

3. Record the elements that are common to both frames. _____

_____

_____

Review Questions

1. What IEEE standard number refers to the Token Ring frame?

   a. 802.2

   b. 802.4

   c. 802.5

   d. 802.1

2. Ethernet is specified by the IEEE 802.3 standard.

   T _____ F _____

3. The portion of a frame that is used to determine if the data was received correctly is the CRC.

   T _____ F _____

4. The source address identifies the MAC address of the sending machine.

   T _____ F _____

5. The destination address identifies the MAC address of the computer receiving the data.

   T _____ F _____

6. In a Token Ring network, Access Control signifies the beginning of the data packet.

   T _____ F _____

7. In an Ethernet network, the Pad portion of a frame pads the frame to a minimum of 46 bytes.

   T _____ F _____

LAB 2.4 DETERMINING THE MAC ADDRESS OF A WINDOWS NT COMPUTER

Objectives

The goal of this lab is to teach you how to determine the MAC address of a Microsoft Windows NT computer. After completing this lab, you will be able to:

➤ Identify the MAC address of a Windows NT computer

➤ Use the IPCONFIG command

Materials Required

This lab will require the following:

➤ A computer with Microsoft Windows NT up and running

ACTIVITY

1. Press **Control + Alt + Delete**. The NT Logon screen appears.

2. Log on as an administrator. The Windows NT desktop appears.

3. Click **Start**, click **Programs**, then click **Command Prompt**. The MS-DOS window appears with the command prompt.

4. Type **IPCONFIG /ALL**, and record the result. _____
   _____
   _____
   _____

5. Type **Exit**. The MS-DOS window closes.

Review Questions

1. What is the purpose of the MAC address? _____
   _____
   _____
   _____

2. The MAC address can be changed with the IPCONFIG command.
   T _____ F _____

3. The MAC address of two computers can be the same.
   T _____ F _____

4. Identify the two main parts of a MAC address.
   _____

5. What is the purpose of the Block ID? _____
   _____
   _____
   _____

6. What information makes up the Device ID? _____
   _____
   _____
   _____

7. The MAC address is synonymous with a logical address.
   T _____ F _____

LAB 2.5 UNDERSTANDING FRAME TYPES

Objectives

The purpose of this lab is to help you understand the importance of choosing the correct frame type when communicating with Novell NetWare servers. After completing this lab you will be able to:

➤ Identify incompatible frame types

Materials Required

In this lab, you will need two computers running different operating systems: one running NetWare 5.0, and the other running Windows NT Server 4.0. The Windows NT server should have GSNW (Gateway Services for NetWare) installed so that the NT server can connect to the NetWare 5.0 server. The material required for this lab consists of the following:

➤ One computer running Novell NetWare 5.0 Server with an internal network number of 13 and a network number of A

➤ One computer running Microsoft Windows NT 4.0 Server with NWLink IPX/SPX Compatible Transport protocol loaded and bound to the NIC

➤ Microsoft GSNW (Gateway Services for NetWare) loaded on the Windows NT computer

ACTIVITY

1. On the Windows NT computer, press **Control + Alt + Delete**. The NT Logon screen appears.

2. Log on as an administrator. The NT desktop appears.

3. On the Windows NT computer, right-click **Network Neighborhood**, and then click **Properties**. The Network screen appears.

4. Click **Protocols**. The Protocols dialog box appears.

5. In the Protocols dialog box, click **NWLink IPX/SPX Compatible Transport**. The entry is highlighted.

6. Click **Properties**. The NWLink IPX/SPX Properties dialog box opens, with the General tab selected.

7. In the General tab, change the internal network number to **13**.

8. Select the adapter type that is on the same physical segment as the Novell server.

9. Click **Manual Frame Type Detection**. In the next step, you will manually select the frame type.

10. Click **Add**. The Manual Frame Detection dialog box appears. In this dialog box, you can select a frame type and a network number.

11. Click **Ethernet 802.3** in the Frame type list box. Selecting this frame type will prevent the Windows NT server from communicating with the Novell 5.0 server, since the Novell server defaults to 802.2 frame types.

12. In the Network Number text box, enter **A**. This is the same network number as the Novell 5.0 server. Click **Add** to create the frame type and network number and to close the Manual Frame Detection dialog box. Click **OK** to close the NWLink IPX/SPX Properties dialog box.

13. Click **Yes** when prompted to reboot.

14. Once the Windows NT server has rebooted, double-click the **Network Neighborhood** icon, double-click **Entire Network**, and then double-click **NetWare or Compatible Network**.

15. Can you see the Novell server in Network Neighborhood? _____

Lab Notes

A Novell 4.x and higher server, running IPX, will use 802.2 frame types by default.

A Novell server running a version of the NOS lower than 4.x along with IPX will use 802.3 frame types by default.

A Novell server running TCP/IP will use Ethernet_II as the frame type.

Review Questions

1. What is the purpose of selecting a frame type on a Novell server?

   _____

   _____

2. Two Novell servers with the same frame type will never be able to communicate.
   T _____ F _____

3. What is the default frame type for a Novell 4.11 server running IPX? _____

4. What is the default frame type for a Novell 5.0 server running IPX? _____

NETWORK PROTOCOLS

Labs included in this chapter

➤ Lab 3.1 Using Address Resolution Protocol (ARP)

➤ Lab 3.2 Removing and Reinstalling the TCP/IP Protocol on a Windows NT Server Computer

➤ Lab 3.3 Unbinding the TCP/IP Protocol on a Novell NetWare 5.0 Server

➤ Lab 3.4 Changing the Binding Order on a Network That Is Using Multiple Protocols

➤ Lab 3.5 Disabling Unnecessary Protocols

LAB 3.1 USING ADDRESS RESOLUTION PROTOCOL (ARP)

Objectives

The goal of this lab is to help you learn about the Address Resolution Protocol, or ARP. After completing this lab, you will be able to:

➤ View the ARP cache

➤ Place an IP address to MAC address mapping in the ARP cache

➤ Understand the purpose of ARP

Materials Required

This lab requires the following:

➤ Two networked computers running Microsoft Windows NT 4.0 Server or Workstation

➤ TCP/IP running on both computers

ACTIVITY

1. Log on to both computers.

2. On each computer, click **Start**, point to **Programs**, and then click **Command Prompt**. The MS-DOS Command Prompt screen appears, displaying the D:\> prompt. (Your command prompt may be another letter, such as C:.)

3. Type **IPCONFIG**. The TCP/IP settings for your computer are displayed.

4. Record the IP address of each computer:

   Computer One: _____   Computer Two: _____.

5. At computer one, type **arp –a**. You may see a mapping of IP addresses to MAC (physical) addresses, as shown in Figure 3-1. This mapping is stored in the ARP cache. Otherwise, you will see a message indicating that no entries are found in the ARP cache.

```
D:\>arp -a

Interface: 160.100.100.112 on Interface 3
  Internet Address        Physical Address        Type
  160.100.100.22          00-e0-29-22-eb-b6       dynamic

D:\>
```

Figure 3-1 Results of the ARP command

6. At computer one, type **PING** followed by the IP address of computer two. For example, if the IP address of computer two is 160.100.100.200, you would type PING 160.100.100.200. This command sends a TCP/IP message to computer two, requesting the MAC address of the second computer's NIC.

7. Type **arp –a** again.

8. Record the result. _____

> The ARP cache is a database that maps IP addresses (Internet addresses) to their corresponding MAC addresses (physical addresses). An ARP cache entry will remain in memory a maximum of 10 minutes. If the entry is not used within 2 minutes, it is deleted.

Review Questions

1. "ARP" stands for "Active Resource Program."
   T _____ F _____

2. The purpose of the ARP cache is to maintain the IP to MAC address mappings.
   T _____ F _____

3. If an entry is not used within 3 minutes, it will be deleted from the ARP cache.
   T _____ F _____

4. ARP is a part of the IPX/SPX protocol.
   T _____ F _____

5. What is the purpose of ARP? _____
   _____
   _____
   _____

6. ARP operates at the Application layer of the OSI Model.
   T _____ F _____

LAB 3.2 REMOVING AND REINSTALLING THE TCP/IP PROTOCOL ON A WINDOWS NT SERVER COMPUTER

Objectives

The goal of this lab is to help you learn about removing and installing the TCP/IP protocol. After completing this lab, you will be able to:

➤ Remove the TCP/IP protocol from a computer

➤ Install the TCP/IP protocol from the I386 folder on the hard disk

➤ Set IP address and subnet mask properties for a Windows NT Server computer

Materials Required

This lab requires the following:

➤ One computer with Microsoft Windows NT 4.0 Server installed

➤ The Microsoft Windows NT 4.0 Server installation CD

ACTIVITY

1. Log on to the Microsoft Windows NT 4.0 Server computer.

2. Insert the Microsoft Windows NT 4.0 Server installation CD in the CD-ROM drive. When the CD Installation screen appears, click the **Browse the CD** button. Locate the I386 folder on the CD and copy it to your hard drive. Close all folders.

3. Right-click the **Network Neighborhood** icon and then click **Properties**. The Network dialog box opens.

4. Click the **Protocol** tab and then click **TCP/IP Protocol**. The TCP/IP Protocol entry is highlighted.

5. Click **Remove**. A warning message appears, indicating that the action is permanent.

6. Click **Yes**.

7. Click **Close**. The TCP/IP protocol is removed and the Network Settings Change dialog box appears, indicating that you must shut down and restart before the new settings take effect.

8. Click **Yes** to restart the computer.

9. Once the computer has restarted, log on as Administrator.

10. Right-click the **Network Neighborhood** icon and then click **Properties**. The Network dialog box opens.

11. Click the **Protocol** tab and then click **Add**. The Select Network Protocol dialog box opens.

12. Select **TCP/IP Protocol** in the Select Network Protocol list and then click **OK**. The TCP/IP Setup dialog box opens.

13. Click **No**. The Windows NT Setup dialog box appears.

14. In the text box, type the path to the I386 folder on the drive C. (For example, type C:\I386.) Click **Continue**. The Setup program installs the TCP/IP protocol suite.

15. Click **Close**.

16. The Microsoft TCP/IP Properties dialog box opens, as shown in Figure 3-2. Here you can enter the computer's IP address and subnet mask properties.

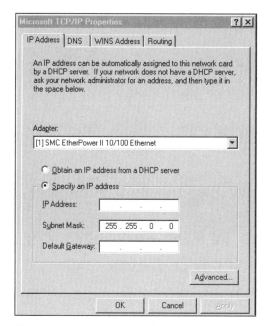

Figure 3-2 The Microsoft TCP/IP Properties dialog.

17. Click the **Specify an IP address** option button. The IP Address, Subnet Mask and Default Gateway text boxes become enabled.

18. Type **170.100.100.105** as the IP address for your computer in the **IP Address** text box.

19. Click the **Subnet Mask** text box. A default subnet mask appears. Record the default subnet mask:_____.

20. Click **OK**. You see a dialog box indicating that you must restart your computer before the changes can take effect.

21. Click **Yes** to restart your computer. After you computer has restarted, test your IP configuration, as explained in the following steps.

22. Click **Start** and then click **Run**. The **Run** dialog box appears.

23. Type **IPCONFIG**. The IP address and subnet mask that you noted in Steps 17 and 18 should appear.

Review Questions

1. TCP/IP stands for Technical Computer Protocol/Internet Protocol.
   T _____ F _____

2. In order for two Windows NT computers to be able to communicate, one must run TCP/IP and the other NetBEUI.
   T _____ F _____

3. TCP/IP is made up of a suite of several protocols.
   T _____ F _____

4. An example of a TCP/IP address is EF-45-A3-55-F3-A2.
   T _____ F _____

5. List the steps required to add another protocol, such as NetBEUI, to a Windows NT computer.

6. NetBEUI is a fast and routable protocol.
   T _____ F _____

7. TCP/IP is a routable protocol.
   T _____ F _____

LAB 3.3 UNBINDING THE TCP/IP PROTOCOL ON A NOVELL NETWARE 5.0 SERVER

Objectives

The goal of this lab is to help you learn how to unbind the TCP/IP protocol on a Novell NetWare 5.0 Server. After completion of this lab, you will be able to:

➤ Explain the necessity of binding protocols

➤ Bind and unbind the TCP/IP protocol on a Novell NetWare 5.0 Server

Materials Required

This lab requires the following:

➤ A computer running Novell NetWare 5.0 Server, running the TCP/IP protocol with an IP Address of 165.100.100.100

➤ A Windows 95 or Windows 98 computer running the TCP/IP protocol, with the Client 32 software loaded

➤ An administrative user account on both computers

➤ All necessary networking equipment to allow the computers to communicate on a network

➤ A NIC driver named SMCPWRII

ACTIVITY

1. Log on to the Windows 95 or Windows 98 computer as the Administrator.

2. Click **Start**, point to **Programs**, and then click **MS–DOS Prompt**. The MS-DOS Prompt window opens.

3. Type **PING 165.100.100.100.** You should see four reply statements listing the IP address of the computer you are pinging, the number of bytes sent, the time in milliseconds and the Time To Live, or TTL value.

4. Go to the Novell server computer, and type **unbind ip from SMCPWRII** at the Novell Server prompt. A screen similar to Figure 3-3 appears.

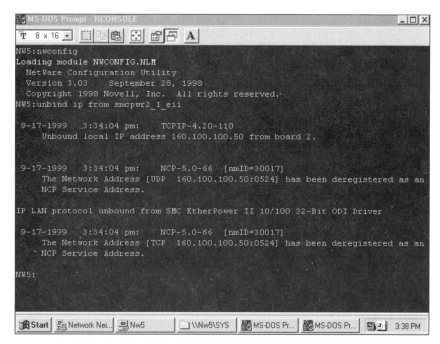

Figure 3-3   Unbinding the IP protocol from the NIC

5. At the Windows 95/98 client computer, attempt to ping the Novell NetWare 5.0 Server again, as in Step 3. Record the result:

_____

6. At the Novell server, bind the IP protocol to the NIC again by typing the following: **bind ip to SMCPWRII addr=165.100.100.100 mask=255.255.0.0.**

7. Attempt to ping the server from the client computer. Record the result:

_____

Review Questions

1. A protocol is bound to the motherboard.

   T _____ F _____

2. Binding is the act of associating a protocol to a NIC.

   T _____ F _____

3. If a protocol is not bound to a NIC, the computer cannot be accessed over the network.

   T _____ F _____

4. If you used Novell's proprietary protocol on a Novell Server, what protocol would you need to install?

   a. NetBEUI

   b. TCP/IP

   c. IPX/SPX

   d. AppleTalk

5. What protocol would you install on a Windows NT computer if you wanted to access a Novell server that was using IPX/SPX?

   a. IPX/SPX

   b. NW Link

   c. AppleTalk

   d. TCP/IP

6. What is the default protocol for Macintosh computers?

   a. NW Link

   b. AppleTalk

   c. TCP/IP

   d. IPX/SPX

Binding is the process of associating a protocol to a NIC. A protocol must be bound to a computer's NIC before the computer can communicate with other computers on a network.

LAB 3.4 CHANGING THE BINDING ORDER ON A MULTIPLE PROTOCOL NETWORK

Objectives

The goal of this lab is to help you understand how the binding order affects network performance. After completion of this lab, you will be able to do the following:

➤ Change the protocol binding order on Microsoft Windows NT 4.0 computers

➤ Discuss how the binding order affects network performance

Materials Required

This lab requires the following:

➤ One Microsoft NT 4.0 Server computer running TCP/IP, NW Link, and NetBEUI

➤ One Microsoft NT 4.0 Workstation computer running TCP/IP, NW Link, and NetBEUI

➤ All networking equipment necessary to allow the computers to communicate on a network

ACTIVITY

1. Log on to the Windows NT 4.0 Workstation computer as an Administrator.

2. Right-click the **Network Neighborhood** icon and click **Properties**. The Network dialog box opens.

3. Click the **Bindings** tab. You see a list of the services that are running on your computer. Among these services, you should see a Server and a Workstation service. In Windows NT, a service is bound to a protocol, and then the protocol is bound to a NIC. The Server service is for incoming requests, while the Workstation service handles outgoing requests.

4. Double-click the **Workstation** service. The protocols that are installed on your computer are displayed, as shown in Figure 3-4.

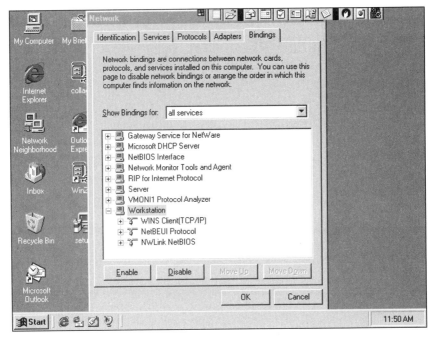

Figure 3-4 Protocol bindings for the Workstation service

5. Record the binding order on your computer: _____

    _____

    _____

    _____

6. Click the protocol on the bottom of the list, and then click the **Move Up** button until the protocol is at the top of the list. (For example, in Figure 3-4, you would click NWLink NetBIOS.)

7. Click **OK**. The changes are written to the Registry.

8. Click **Yes** when prompted to restart your computer.

9. Log on again and check your bindings now. Record the new binding order: _____

    _____

    _____

    _____

10. Set your binding order to reflect the original settings you recorded in Step 5.

Review Questions

1. On a Microsoft network, services are bound to protocols and protocols are bound to NICs.

    T _____ F _____

2. If you have both the NetBEUI and TCP/IP protocols bound to the Workstation service of your NT computer, what would you suggest as the binding order?

3. On a Microsoft Windows NT network, you can only change the binding order at the server computer.

   T _____   F _____

4. The binding order affects network performance.

   T _____   F _____

5. You should place the most frequently used protocols at the bottom of the binding list.

   T _____   F _____

6. What is the purpose of binding? _____

   _____

   _____

   _____

Multiple protocols may be bound and running on a computer. To conserve network resources, you should place the most frequently used protocols at the top of the binding list.

LAB 3.5 DISABLING UNNECESSARY PROTOCOLS

Objectives

The goal of this lab is to help you learn how to disable protocols that are not being used. Once you have completed this lab, you will be able to:

➤ Disable unnecessary protocols

➤ Enable necessary protocols

Materials Required

This lab requires the following:

➤ One Microsoft Windows NT 4.0 Server computer with only the NetBEUI protocol

➤ One Microsoft Windows NT 4.0 Workstation computer with only the NetBEUI protocol

➤ All networking equipment necessary to allow the computers to communicate on a network

ACTIVITY

1. Log on to the Windows NT 4.0 Workstation computer as an Administrator.

2. Right-click the **Network Neighborhood** icon and click **Properties**. The Network dialog box opens.

3. Click the **Binding** tab. You see a list of the services that are running on your computer, including a Server and a Workstation service.

4. Double-click the **Server** service. The protocols that are installed on your computer are displayed.

5. Double-click **NetBEUI protocol**. The adapters installed on your computer are displayed. Record the adapters on your computer:

   _____

6. Click an adapter to select it, and then click the **Disable** button. Repeat this step for all adapters.

7. Repeat Steps 4 through 6 for the Workstation service.

8. Click **OK**. The changes are written to the Registry.

9. Click **Yes** when prompted to restart your computer.

10. Log on to the computer.

11. Attempt to connect to the second computer from the computer that has the bindings disabled. Record your findings: _____

   _____

12. Repeat Steps 1 through 5.

13. Repeat Step 6 except click **Enable** to enable the bindings.

14. Repeat Steps 7 through 10.

Review Questions

1. Jack wants to bind the TCP/IP protocol to adapter 1 and the NetBEUI protocol to adapter 2 on his NT Workstation. How should he proceed?

   _____

   _____

   _____

2. If a binding is disabled, the computer cannot be seen on the network.
   T _____ F _____

3. Why would you want to disable a protocol? _____

   _____

   _____

   _____

4. You should always install and bind all available protocols whether you use them or not.
   T _____ F _____

5. You must remove the protocol if you want to temporarily discontinue using it.
   T _____ F _____

6. Why would you ever want to disable an adapter?

NETWORKING MEDIA

LAB 4.1 MEDIA CHARACTERISTICS

Objective

The goal of this lab is to help you learn about different media costs and characteristics. This will give you experience in comparing costs of network components. After completing this lab, you will be able to:

➤ Identify the costs and characteristics of 10BaseT and 10Base2

Materials Required

This lab will require the following:

➤ Access to a retail store that sells computer networking equipment

➤ Pencil and paper

ACTIVITY

1. Visit a retail computer store that sells Ethernet 10BaseT (RJ-45) and 10Base2 (Thinnet or thin coax) cable. Record the name of the retail store.

   _____

2. Record the cost of a Category 5 cable, with an RJ-45 connection, that is at least 10 feet in length. _____

   _____

3. Record the cost of an Ethernet 10-Mbps 4-port hub with an RJ-45 connection. _____

   _____

4. Record the cost of an Ethernet 10-Mbps NIC with an RJ-45 connection.

   _____

5. Record the total cost of the 10BaseT cable, hub, and NIC.

   _____

6. Record the cost of an RG-58 A/U (10Base2 or Thinnet) coaxial cable that is at least 10 feet in length. _____

   _____

7. Record the cost of two terminators. _____

   _____

8. Record the cost of a T-connector. _____

   _____

9. Record the cost of an Ethernet 10-Mbps NIC with a BNC connection.

   _____

10. Record the total cost of the 10Base2 cable, terminators, T-connector, and NIC.

_____

_____

11. Overall, which is more cost-effective, the 10BaseT or the 10Base2 medium?

_____

Review Questions

1. The connector type for a 10BaseT network is RJ-11.

   T _____ F _____

2. A Thicknet cable uses an RG–58 A/U coaxial cable.

   T _____ F _____

3. A 10BaseT network requires a terminator at each end of the network.

   T _____ F _____

4. Define the term attenuation. _____

_____

_____

_____

5. What is the purpose of cable shielding? _____

_____

_____

_____

6. Define the term throughput. _____

_____

_____

_____

7. Which of the following statements about 10Base5 is true? Choose all that apply.

   a. It has a throughput of 10 Mbps.

   b. It has a throughput of 5 Mbps.

   c. It has a maximum segment length of 500 meters.

   d. It has a maximum segment length of 10 meters.

   e. It carries only one signal at a time.

8. What is the maximum throughput of a Category 3 cable?

_____

LAB 4.2 CREATING A 10BASET CROSSOVER CABLE TO CONNECT TWO COMPUTERS

Objectives

The goal of this lab is to teach you how to make your own cable in order create a simple peer-to-peer network. After completing this lab, you will be able to:

➤ Directly connect two computers with an RJ-45 crossover cable by plugging one end of the cable into the NIC of one computer and the other end of the cable into the NIC of the second computer

➤ Use a cable tester to ensure cable integrity

Materials Required

This lab will require the following:

➤ At least 10 feet of Category 5 cable

➤ Two RJ-45 connectors

➤ Two computers running Windows NT with an Ethernet NIC with an RJ-45 connector

➤ A network crimper

➤ A wire stripper

➤ A cable tester

➤ A wire cutting tool

ACTIVITY

1. Use the wire cutter to make a clean cut at both ends of the UTP cable.

2. Use the wire stripper to remove the sheath off one inch (or less) of one end of the UTP cable. Take care not to damage the insulation on the twisted pairs inside.

3. Slightly separate the four wire pairs, but keep the pairs twisted around each other.

4. Use the wire stripper or a penknife to remove approximately 3/8 inch of insulation from each of the eight wires. You will have to untwist the wire pairs to do this, but do not separate the wires in each pair more than a half-inch from each other.

5. Use a crimping tool to connect the wires in the RJ-45 connector, matching their color to their correct pin number as described in Table 4-1. You have now completed one end of the cable.

Table 4-1 Pin numbers and color codes for creating a straight-through cable end

Pin Number	Function	Color
1	Transmit +	White and green
2	Transmit –	Green
3	Receive +	White and orange
4	Not used	Blue
5	Not used	White and blue
6	Receive –	Orange
7	Not used	White and brown
8	Not used	Brown

6. Repeat Steps 1 through 4 for the other end of the twisted pair cable.

7. Use a crimping tool to connect the wires in the RJ-45 connector, matching their color to their correct pin number as described in Table 4-2. This will cross the Transmit and Receive (both positive and negative) wires, which will allow the computers to communicate when connected. After completing this step, your crossover cable will be ready to use.

Table 4-2 Pin numbers and color codes for creating a crossover cable end

Pin Number	Function	Color
1	Transmit +	White and orange
2	Transmit –	Orange
3	Receive +	White and green
4	Not used	Blue
5	Not used	White and blue
6	Receive –	Green
7	Not used	White and brown
8	Not used	Brown

8. Plug each end of the cable into the cable tester. (Refer to Figure 4-1 for an example of a cable being tested with a cable tester.) The lights on the tester should turn on. If not, then recrimp the ends of the cable and repeat Step 1. If the lights turn on, proceed to the next step.

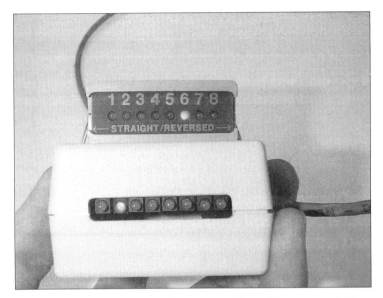

Figure 4-1 Cable tester used to ensure the cable was created correctly

9. Remove the cable ends from the cable tester.

10. Connect one end of the cable to the NIC of one computer.

11. Connect the other end of the same cable to the NIC of the second computer. The lights on each NIC will turn on.

12. On one computer, press **Control+Alt+Delete**. The NT Logon screen appears.

13. Enter an Administrator username and password, and click **OK**. The Windows NT desktop appears.

14. Double-click the **Network Neighborhood** icon. The Network screen appears with the name of the other computer.

15. Double-click the icon for the other computer. Do you see a list of folders for the other computer? _____

16. Log off the computer.

Review Questions

1. Define the purpose of a crossover cable. _____

_____

_____

_____

2. You always need a hub in order to connect two computers in a 10BaseT network.
   T _____ F _____

3. Draw lines connecting the pins of End 1 to the pins of End 2, to indicate a configuration that would allow a crossover cable to operate properly.

   <u>End 1</u>   <u>End 2</u>

   Pin 1   Pin 1

   Pin 2   Pin 2

   Pin 3   Pin 3

   Pin 4   Pin 4

   Pin 5   Pin 5

   Pin 6   Pin 6

   Pin 7   Pin 7

   Pin 8   Pin 8

4. Category 3 cable can operate at speeds of 100 Mbps.
   T _____ F _____

5. Why are the wires twisted on an STP cable? _____
   _____
   _____
   _____

6. Discuss the differences between STP and UTP. _____
   _____
   _____
   _____

7. What is meant by the phrase twist ratio? _____
   _____
   _____
   _____

LAB 4.3 COMPARING MEDIA TYPES

Objectives

The goal of this lab is to help you learn more about wire-bound and wireless media types. You will choose a type of media from each category, identify its characteristics, advantages and disadvantages and discuss a business scenario in which it might be used. You will then compare the two media types. After completing this lab, you will be able to:

➤ Identify the characteristics, advantages and disadvantages of a wire-bound media type and a wireless media type

➤ Identify the differences between wire-bound and wireless media types

Materials Required

This lab will require the following:

➤ Pencil and paper

ACTIVITY

1. Decide on a type of wire-bound media to discuss. Record the type you choose, its characteristics, advantages and disadvantages, and a situation in which it could be used. _____

_____
_____
_____
_____
_____
_____

2. Decide on a type of wireless media type to discuss. Record the type you choose, its characteristics, advantages and disadvantages, and a situation in which it could be used. _____

_____
_____
_____
_____
_____
_____

3. Compare the two media types you discussed in the previous two steps and record your result. In your discussion, consider whether one has a particular advantage or disadvantage as compared to the other. _____

_____
_____
_____
_____
_____

4. If you were a network project manager, which media type would you use and why? _____

_____

_____

Review Questions

1. What type of signaling do wireless LANs typically use? Choose all that apply.

   a. coaxial

   b. infrared

   c. fiber

   d. radio frequency

   e. 10BaseT

2. A 100Base5 network works on "line of sight" transmission.

   T _____ F _____

3. RF would be a good medium for locations that are subject to heavy EMI.

   T _____ F _____

4. Which of the following are characteristics of a Thicknet network? Choose all that apply.

   a. vampire taps

   b. transceiver cable

   c. RJ-45 cable

   d. infrared cable

5. Indirect infrared transmission bounces signals off walls, the ceiling, and other objects.

   T _____ F _____

6. Radio frequency transmission broadcasts over certain frequencies, similar to the way radio and television broadcasts operate.

   T _____ F _____

7. Which type of RF technology concentrates energy at a single frequency? Choose the correct answer.

   a. spread spectrum

   b. direct infrared

   c. indirect infrared

   d. narrowband

   e. broadband

8. A plenum grade cable is more fire-resistant than other cable types.

   T _____ F _____

LAB 4.4 UNDERSTANDING HOW AN INCORRECTLY MADE 10BaseT CABLE FAILS

Objective

The goal of this lab is to help you understand why the placement of the wires in a 10BaseT cable is so important. After completing this lab, you will be able to:

➤ Identify the problem associated with an incorrectly wired 10BaseT cable

Materials Required

This lab will require the following:

➤ At least 10 feet of Category 5 cable

➤ Four RJ-45 connectors

➤ Two computers running Windows NT, using an Ethernet NIC with an RJ-45 connector

➤ A network crimper

➤ A wire stripper

➤ A wire cutting tool

ACTIVITY

1. Complete Steps 1 through 5 of Project 4.2, earlier in this chapter. When finished, you will have completed one end of the cable.

2. Repeat Steps 1 through 4 of Project 4.2 for the other end of the twisted pair cable.

3. Using a crimping tool, connect the wires in the RJ-45 connector, matching their color to their correct pin number, as described in Table 4–3. This results in an incorrectly made cable.

4. Connect the ends of the cable to each computer. The network adapter lights on each computer will not turn on. If they do, you accidentally made a correctly wired cable, and you need to begin this lab again. If they do not turn on, proceed with the next step.

5. On one computer, press **Control+Alt+Delete**. The NT Logon screen appears.

6. Enter an Administrator username and password, and click **OK**. The Windows NT desktop appears.

Table 4-3 Pin numbers and color codes for creating an incorrect cable end

Pin Number	Function	Color
1	Transmit +	Brown
2	Transmit −	White and brown
3	Receive +	White and blue
4	Not used	White and orange
5	Not used	Orange
6	Receive −	Blue
7	Not used	White and green
8	Not used	Green

4

7. Double-click the **Network Neighborhood** icon. The Network screen appears.

8. Can you see the other computer in the list? _____

9. Log off the computer.

10. Using the wire cutting tool, cut the end of the cable about an inch from the RJ-45 connector. The RJ-45 connector should drop off.

11. Rewire and recrimp the cable by following Steps 1 through 6 of Project 4.2 of the textbook.

12. Repeat Step 7 again.

13. Does the second computer appear in the list now? _____

Review Questions

1. Which pin number is used for transmitting a positive signal on an RJ-45 cable?

    a. 1

    b. 2

    c. 3

    d. 4

    e. 5

2. Define the term bend radius. _____

    _____

    _____

    _____

3. Which category of cable can support 16-Mbps Token Ring? Choose the best answer.

   a. Category 1

   b. Category 2

   c. Category 3

   d. Category 4

   e. Category 8

4. What is the purpose of a crimper? _____

   _____

   _____

   _____

5. List the organizations that set twisted-pair wiring standards. _____

   _____

   _____

   _____

6. The standard number that specifies the wiring characteristics for twisted-pair wiring is TIA/EIA 568.

   T _____ F _____

LAB 4.5 UNDERSTANDING CABLE TYPES

Objective

The goal of this lab is to help you understand the necessity of using the correct cable type for a given hub. After completing this lab, you will be able to:

➤ Identify the proper cable type for a particular hub

Materials Required

This lab will require the following:

➤ A computer running Microsoft Windows NT 4.0, but *not* attached to a network

➤ A second computer running Microsoft Windows NT 4.0, that *is* attached to the network with a correct cable. This computer should be plugged into a port on the hub, and both the computer and hub should be operating properly

➤ An Ethernet 100-Mbps NIC inside each computer

➤ An Ethernet 100-Mbps hub

➤ At least 10 feet of Category 3 cable

ACTIVITY

1. Using the Category 3 cable, complete Steps 1 through 6 of Project 4.2. Unlike in the preceding project, you should be certain to create the cable correctly.

2. Plug one end of the cable to the NIC of the first Windows NT computer and the other end into the hub. The lights should not turn on.

3. Explain why the lights do not turn on. _____

   _____

   _____

4. Record what would you do in order to correct this situation. _____

   _____

   _____

Review Questions

1. Discuss the differences between Category 3 and Category 5 cable.

    _____

    _____

    _____

2. Enhanced Category 5 has a lower twist ratio than regular Category 5 cable.
   T _____ F _____

3. Category 5 cable is about 6 times faster than Category 6 cable.
   T _____ F _____

4. Category 3 cable has been used with 10-Mbps Ethernet and 4-Mbps Token Ring networks.
   T _____ F _____

5. The outer part of twisted-pair cabling is called the jacket or sheath.
   T _____ F _____

6. Which category of cable contains two wire pairs and is best suited for voice communications?

   a. Category 5

   b. Enhanced Category 5

   c. Category 1

   d. Category 4

   e. Category 9

7. High-quality Category 5 cable can transmit up to 1 Gbps.
   T _____ F _____

NETWORK ARCHITECTURE

Labs included in this chapter

➤ Lab 5.1 LAN Topologies

➤ Lab 5.2 The Bus Topology

➤ Lab 5.3 Understanding Switching

➤ Lab 5.4 Using Network Monitor to View Data Packets

➤ Lab 5.5 The Star Topology

LAB 5.1 LAN TOPOLOGIES

Objectives

The goal of this lab is to help you learn about bus, ring, and star topologies. After completing this lab, you will be able to:

➤ Identify a bus, ring, and star topology

➤ Identify the advantages and disadvantages of bus, ring, and star topologies

Materials Required

This lab will require the following:

➤ Pencil and paper

ACTIVITY

1. Draw a bus topology. Use a letter "T" for placement of a terminator.

2. Draw a ring topology.

3. Draw a star topology. Use a letter "H" for placement of a hub.

4. Record the advantages and disadvantages of a bus topology. _____
   _____
   _____
   _____

5. Record the advantages and disadvantages of a ring topology. _____
   _____
   _____
   _____

6. Record the advantages and disadvantages of a star topology. _____

_____

_____

_____

Review Questions

1. In a star topology, all the wires from all the computers are connected to a hub.

   T _____ F _____

2. In a ring topology, nodes communicate by passing a token to each other.

   T _____ F _____

3. Which topology incorporates a cable from each node to a central device?

   a. bus

   b. ring

   c. star

   d. enterprise

4. In which topology is a single computer capable of bringing down the entire network?

   a. bus

   b. ring

   c. star

   d. enterprise

5. Define the term hybrid topology. _____

   _____

   _____

   _____

6. Compare a star-wired ring topology with a star-wired bus topology.

   _____

   _____

   _____

LAB 5.2 THE BUS TOPOLOGY

Objectives

The goal of this lab is to teach you about the importance of terminators in a bus topology. After completing this lab, you will be able to:

➤ Explain what happens when a bus network is not terminated

Materials Required

This lab will require the following:

➤ Two booted Windows NT computers, with working NICs, arranged in a bus topology

➤ The necessary coaxial cable and T-connectors to connect the two computers

➤ Two terminators inserted at the two ends of the coaxial cable

ACTIVITY

1. Log on to one computer as an Administrator. The Windows NT desktop appears.

2. Double-click the **Network Neighborhood** icon. The Network screen appears with the name of the other computer.

3. Exit Network Neighborhood.

4. Unscrew the terminator on one end of the network.

5. Double-click the **Network Neighborhood** icon again. This time the Network screen with the other computer's name no longer appears. Instead, an hourglass appears, indicating that Windows NT is searching for the computer. After a few minutes, an error message dialog box will appear indicating the computer could not be found.

6. Click **OK** to close the error message dialog box.

7. Exit Network Neighborhood.

8. Reinsert the terminator and repeat Step 2 above.

9. Log off.

Review Questions

1. What is the purpose of a terminator? _____
   _____
   _____
   _____

2. If both terminators are missing from the ends of the cable in bus topology, the network will function properly.
   T _____ F _____

3. A star topology always uses a terminator.
   T _____ F _____

4. Which of the following topologies uses a terminator? Choose the best answer.

   a. star

   b. ring

   c. bus

   d. star–wired ring

LAB 5.3 UNDERSTANDING SWITCHING

5

Objectives

The goal of this lab is to help you learn more about circuit, message, and packet switching. After completing this lab, you will be able to:

➤ Identify the characteristics of circuit, message, and packet switching

Materials Required

This lab will require the following:

➤ Pencil and paper

ACTIVITY

1. Discuss circuit switching and include at least two examples of technologies that use it. _____

   _____

   _____

   _____

2. Discuss message switching and include at least one example of a technology that uses it. _____

   _____

   _____

   _____

3. Discuss packet switching and include at least two examples of technologies that use it. _____

   _____

   _____

   _____

Review Questions

1. Circuit switching uses a "store and forward" mechanism to send data from one device to another.

   T _____ F _____

2. Which type of switching method uses a dedicated path to send and receive data?

    a. circuit

    b. packet

    c. message

    d. e-mail

3. Which switching technique breaks data into smaller units?

    a. circuit

    b. packet

    c. message

    d. ATM

4. In message switching, the device that receives the message must have enough RAM capacity and CPU capability to manage the message.
T _____ F _____

5. In packet switching, each packet contains a sequence number for the packet.
T _____ F _____

6. Packet switching is suitable for live audio or video conferencing.
T _____ F _____

7. In message switching, all data flows along the same path.
T _____ F _____

8. Which type of switching method does an e-mail application use?

    a. circuit

    b. packet

    c. message

    d. token

LAB 5.4 USING NETWORK MONITOR TO VIEW DATA PACKETS

Objective

The intent of this lab is to further your understanding of how data packets are arranged. After completing this lab, you will be able to:

➤ Identify the portions of a data packet

➤ Use Microsoft's Network Monitor utility

Materials Required

This lab will require the following:

➤ One Microsoft Windows NT 4.0 Server computer and one Microsoft Windows NT 4.0 Workstation computer with the following protocols loaded and bound to the NICs of both computers: TCP/IP, NW Link IPX/SPX Compatible Transport, and NetBEUI

➤ Microsoft Network Monitor Tools and Agent installed on the Windows NT server

ACTIVITY

1. Log on to the Windows NT Server computer, as an Administrator. The Windows NT desktop appears.

2. Click **Start**, point to **Programs**, point to **Administrative Tools**, and then click **Network Monitor**. The Network Monitor window opens.

3. Click **Capture**, and then click **Start**. Network Monitor begins capturing data packets.

4. On the Windows NT Workstation computer, log on as Administrator and double-click the icon for the Windows NT Server computer in Network Neighborhood. Try to view the contents of a folder on the Windows NT Server computer. The point of this step is to generate enough activity to produce a good sample representation of captured data in Network Monitor. Repeat this step for at least 1 minute.

5. Go back to Network Monitor, click **Capture**, and click **Stop**.

6. Click **Capture**, and then click **Display Captured Data**. The Network Monitor Capture Summary window opens, showing information on captured data arranged in rows and columns, as shown in Figure 5-1.

7. Locate an LLC entry in the Protocol column.

8. Double-click on an Ethernet 802.3 entry.

9. Identify the MAC address of the destination computer in Figure 5-1. Record the result: _____

10. Locate the MAC address of the source computer for your captured data. Record the result: _____

11. Exit Network Monitor without saving the captured data.

12. Log off both computers.

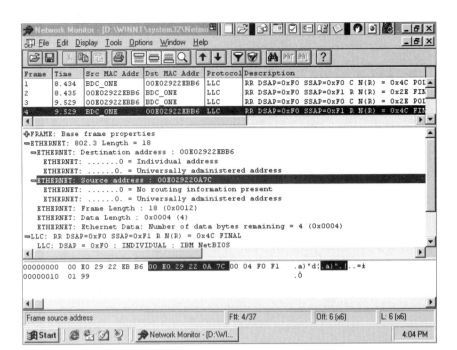

Figure 5-1 Data captured in Network Monitor

Review Questions

1. What is the purpose of the checksum? _____

_____

_____

_____

2. How many times is a checksum calculated when a packet of data is sent
   from a source to a destination computer?

   a. 1

   b. 2

   c. 3

   d. 4

3. What is the purpose of a sequence number? _____

_____

_____

_____

4. Define the term CSMA/CD. _____

_____

_____

_____

5. What is the purpose of the source address and destination address in a frame?

_____

_____

6. What is the purpose of the LLC in an Ethernet 802.2 frame? _____

_____

_____

7. Ethernet 802.3 does not support an LLC field.
   T _____ F _____

5

LAB 5.5 THE STAR TOPOLOGY

Objective

This lab will help you understand how to create a star topology. You will connect two computers to separate hubs and then connect the hubs. After completing this lab, you will be able to:

➤ Create a star topology network

Materials Required

This lab will require the following:

➤ One Microsoft Windows NT 4.0 Server computer and one Microsoft Windows NT 4.0 Workstation computer with the following protocols loaded and bound to the NICs of both computers: TCP/IP, NWLink IPX/SPX Compatible Transport, and NetBEUI

➤ Two Ethernet 10/100 8-port hubs with a crossover or uplink port

➤ Three Category 5 twisted-pair cables, either purchased at a computer store or created by following the steps in Project 4.2, in Chapter 4 of this manual

ACTIVITY

1. Power on the two computers and the two hubs.

2. Connect one end of one cable to port 5 of one of the hubs, and connect the other end of the same cable to the Windows NT Server computer's NIC. The lights on port 5 of the hub and on the Windows NT Server computer's NIC should turn on. (On some devices, the lights will flicker on and off; this is normal activity.)

3. Repeat the previous step for the Windows NT Workstation computer.

4. Connect the third cable to the uplink port of one hub and to port 1 of the second hub. After you connect the two hubs, you should see lights on the uplink port of the first hub and on port 1 of the second hub.

5. On the Windows NT Server computer, log on as an Administrator.

6. Double-click the **Network Neighborhood** icon. The Network screen appears with the name of the workstation. Do you see the Windows NT Workstation computer's name in the list? _____

7. Exit Network Neighborhood.

8. Unplug one of the RJ-45 connectors from one of the ports. What happens to the light on that port? _____

9. Double-click the **Network Neighborhood** icon again. Does the Windows NT Workstation computer's name appear in the list now?

_____

10. Plug the connector back into the port, and exit Network Neighborhood.

Review Questions

1. A bus topology uses a hub to connect all computers.
   T _____ F _____

2. To connect seven computers in a star topology, you would need to use a single cable.
   T _____ F _____

3. Define the purpose of the lights on a hub. _____

   _____

   _____

4. What is the maximum distance in meters of a single UTP cable? Choose the best answer.

   a. 10

   b. 100

   c. 200

   d. 500

5. Which of the following is true regarding the term 100BaseT? Choose all that apply.

   a. It has a speed of 100 megabytes per second.

   b. It has a speed of 100 megabits per second.

   c. It carries a single signal down the cable.

   d. The "T" stands for twisted pair.

   e. The "I" stands for terminator.

6. In a star topology, the failure of a single node will not necessarily bring down the remaining nodes.
   T _____ F _____

CHAPTER SIX

NETWORK HARDWARE

Labs included in this chapter

➤ Lab 6.1 Network Interface Cards (NICs)

➤ Lab 6.2 Creating a Router by Installing Two NICs in a Computer

➤ Lab 6.3 Understanding Hubs

➤ Lab 6.4 Understanding Routing Protocols

➤ Lab 6.5 Understanding Networking Hardware

LAB 6.1 NETWORK INTERFACE CARDS (NICS)

Objective

The goal of this lab is to help you learn about network interface cards (NICs). After completing this lab, you will be able to:

➤ Understand the characteristics of various NICs

Materials Required

This lab will require the following:

➤ Pencil and paper

ACTIVITY

1. Define the term Industry Standard Architecture. _____

   _____

   _____

   _____

2. Define the term Micro Channel Architecture. _____

   _____

   _____

   _____

3. Define the term Extended Industry Standard Architecture. _____

   _____

   _____

   _____

4. Define the term Peripheral Component Interconnect. _____

   _____

   _____

   _____

5. Draw a side view of the four types of NICs. Be sure to label each drawing.

6. List the stages in transmission of data from the motherboard to the network cable on a PC.

Review Questions

1. The capacity of a data bus is measured by the number of bits it can transfer and by its speed.
   T _____ F _____

2. Explain how the data bus relates to a NIC. _____
   _____
   _____
   _____

3. IBM developed MCA for its PS/2 line of computers.
   T _____ F _____

4. An MCA NIC is compatible with an EISA slot on a motherboard.
   T _____ F _____

5. An ISA NIC is faster than a PCI NIC.
   T _____ F _____

6. What type of computer uses a PCMCIA NIC? _____
   _____

7. Some PCs support multiple bus types.
   T _____ F _____

8. Identify three popular NIC vendors. _____
   _____

9. What is the purpose of the IRQ?
   _____
   _____
   _____

LAB 6.2 CREATING A ROUTER BY INSTALLING TWO NICS IN A COMPUTER

Objectives

The goal of this lab is to teach you how to create a router by installing two NICs in a computer. You will also install the network adapter drivers and set the TCP/IP properties of each NIC. After completing this lab, you will be able to:

➤ Transform a PC into a router by installing two NICs

➤ Set TCP/IP properties on each NIC

Materials Required

This lab will require the following:

➤ A PC running Windows NT Server 4.0 with at least two bus slots available

➤ Two PCI NICs with RJ-45 connectors

➤ Two Ethernet 100-Mbps hubs

➤ Two Category 5 STP or UTP cables (noncrossover)

➤ The Windows NT Server 4.0 installation CD

➤ The NICs' device driver on the Windows NT Server installation CD

➤ A toolkit with a Phillips-head screwdriver, a ground mat, and a ground strap

ACTIVITY

1. Power off the computer.

2. Unplug the power cord from the computer.

3. Place the ground strap on your wrist and attach it to the ground strap underneath the computer.

4. Remove any screws from the computer's case.

5. Remove the computer case.

6. Choose a vacant PCI slot on the system board where you will insert the NIC. Remove the metal slot cover from the slot you will use.

7. Place the NIC in the slot.

8. Attach the NIC to the system unit with the Phillips-head screwdriver. This will secure the NIC in place.

9. Replace the cover.

10. Reinsert the screws on the cover.

11. Plug in the computer and turn it on.

12. Connect one end of one cable to one NIC. Connect the other end of the same cable to one of the hubs.

13. Connect one end of the second cable to the second NIC. Connect the other end of the same cable to the second hub.

14. Log on as Administrator. The Windows NT Desktop appears.

15. Right-click on **Network Neighborhood** and then click **Properties**. The Network dialog box appears, with the Identification tab highlighted by default.

16. Click **Adapters**. The Network Adapters dialog box appears.

17. Click **Add**. A list of NIC drivers appears.

18. Use the scroll bar to locate your NIC.

19. Click the name of the NIC. The entry is highlighted.

20. Click **OK**. The Windows NT Setup dialog box appears.

21. Insert the Windows NT Server installation CD into the CD-ROM drive.

22. Click **Continue**. The NIC driver appears in the Network Adapter list.

23. Click **Close**. The drivers are copied to the hard disk. Next, the Microsoft TCP/IP Properties dialog box appears.

24. Click **Specify an IP address**. The IP Address, Subnet mask, and Default gateway entries are highlighted.

25. For the IP Address, enter 160.100.100.100.

26. For the Subnet mask, enter 255.255.0.0.

27. Leave the Default gateway blank.

28. Click **OK**. The Network Setup Change dialog box appears.

29. Click **Yes** to restart your computer.

30. Repeat Steps 1 through 29 for the second NIC, except use these TCP/IP properties: IP Address of 170.100.100.100 and a subnet mask of 255.255.0.0, and a leave the default gateway blank.

31. Once the Windows NT Server is running, look at the lights on each NIC. Are they on? _____

32. Look at the port lights on the hub. Are they on? _____

Review Questions

1. What is the purpose of the NIC driver?_____
   _____
   _____
   _____

2. To what OSI layer does a router belong?
   a. Physical
   b. Application
   c. Session
   d. Network
   e. Transport

3. One of the benefits of a router is that it minimizes network congestion.
   T _____ F _____

4. Which of the following protocols cross a router? Choose all that apply.

    a. NetBEUI

    b. TCP/IP

    c. IPX/SPX

    d. AppleTalk

5. A router with multiple slots that can hold different interface cards or other devices is called a modular router.

    T _____ F _____

6. Multiple NICs in a computer can function together as a router.

    T _____ F _____

7. Identify three settings that you may need to set on a NIC._____

_____

_____

_____

8. What is the difference between a router and a hub?_____

_____

_____

_____

> **Note**
> To add a router to your network, you can either purchase a special piece of networking equipment or you can install multiple NICs in a PC, as described in this project.

LAB 6.3 UNDERSTANDING HUBS

Objective

The goal of this lab is to help you learn more about the different types of hubs. After completing this lab, you will be able to:

➤ Identify the characteristics of different hubs

Materials Required

This lab will require the following:

➤ Pencil and paper

ACTIVITY

1. Define the term standalone hubs. _____
   _____
   _____
   _____

2. Define the term stackable hubs. _____
   _____
   _____
   _____

3. Define the term modular hubs. _____
   _____
   _____
   _____

4. Define the term intelligent hubs. _____
   _____
   _____
   _____

Review Questions

1. Define the term MIB. _____
   _____
   _____
   _____

2. A passive hub can access an MIB in order to analyze network performance and problems.
   T _____ F _____

3. Standalone hubs serve a grouping of computers and are therefore suited to small departments, homes, or test lab environments.
   T _____ F _____

4. Stackable hubs connected together logically represent a single large hub to the network.
   T _____ F _____

5. What type of hub provides a number of network interface options in a single chassis?
   a. passive
   b. stackable
   c. modular
   d. standalone

6. On Token Ring hubs, the Collision LED turns on to indicate collisions.
   T _____ F _____

7. Zac's computer is connected to a port on an Ethernet hub. He cannot access his Novell NetWare 5.0 server, which is also connected to a different port on the same hub. Jessie's computer is also connected to a different port on the same hub, and her computer can access the server. Zac notices that the port's light for his network connection is not on. What could be the problem? Choose all that apply.

   a. Zac's computer could be turned off.

   b. The cable may not be plugged into the NIC on Zac's computer.

   c. The hub may be malfunctioning.

   d. The Novell NetWare 5.0 Server may be down.

   e. The cable could have been improperly made.

8. What is the purpose of a port on a hub?_____
   _____
   _____
   _____

9. In order to connect hubs in a daisy-chain fashion, you would use the Uplink port.
   T _____ F _____

LAB 6.4 UNDERSTANDING ROUTING PROTOCOLS

Objectives

The intent of this lab is to increase your knowledge of routing protocols. After completing this lab, you will be able to:

➤ Explain the function of various routing protocols

➤ Install Microsoft's Routing Internet Protocol (RIP)

Materials Required

This lab will require the following:

➤ Two Microsoft Windows NT 4.0 servers with TCP/IP enabled

➤ An IP address of 160.100.100.100, a subnet mask of 255.255.0.0, and a blank default gateway entry for one Windows NT server

➤ An IP Address of 170.100.100.100, a subnet mask of 255.255.0.0, and a blank default gateway entry for the second Windows NT server

➤ One Ethernet 10- or 100-Mbps hub

➤ An NIC installed in each Windows NT server

➤ A twisted-pair cable connecting each computer to the hub

➤ One Microsoft Windows NT 4.0 Server installation CD

ACTIVITY

1. Logon as Administrator on one of the Windows NT Server computers. The Windows NT Desktop appears.

2. Right-click on **Network Neighborhood** and then click **Properties**. The Network dialog box appears with the Identification tab selected by default.

3. Click **Services**. A list of installed services appears.

4. Click **Add**. The **Select Network Service** dialog box appears.

5. Use the scroll bar to locate **RIP for Internet Protocol** in the list of available services.

6. Click **OK**. The Windows NT Setup dialog box appears with the drive letter of the CD-ROM drive and the I386 folder name.

7. Insert the Windows NT Server installation CD into the CD-ROM drive.

8. Click **Continue**. The drivers are copied to the Windows NT Server computer.

9. Click **Close**. The Network Settings Change dialog box appears.

10. Click **Yes** to reboot the computer. Once the computer is up and running again, Windows NT setup installs RIP for IP.

11. Repeat Steps 1 through 10 for the second Windows NT Server computer. Once RIP for IP is installed on both computers, they will dynamically share their routing tables.

Review Questions

1. Micki has two Novell NetWare 4.11 servers that are running the IPX/SPX protocol. She wants them to share their routing information. What should each Novell server run?

   a. RIP for IP

   b. RIP for IPX

   c. RIP for AppleTalk

   d. OSPF

2. In order to determine the best path to transfer data, routers communicate using routing protocols such as TCP/IP.

   T _____ F _____

6

3. Define the term convergence time. _____
   _____
   _____
   _____

4. Which routing protocol is used for Internet backbones?

   a. OSPF

   b. RIP for IP

   c. EIGRP

   d. TCP/IP

   e. BGP

5. The term best path refers to the optimal route from one node on one network to another node on a different network.

   T _____ F _____

6. Which protocol was developed by Cisco Systems and has a fast convergence time but is supported only on Cisco routers?

   a. OSPF

   b. RIP for IP

   c. EIGRP

   d. TCP/IP

   e. BGP

7. Compare RIP to OSPF. _____
   _____
   _____
   _____

LAB 6.5 UNDERSTANDING NETWORKING HARDWARE

Objective

The intent of this lab is to help you understand different networking hardware. After completing this lab, you will be able to:

➤ Identify the purpose of networking hardware

Materials Required

In this lab, you will need the following:

➤ Pencil and paper

ACTIVITY

1. Define the term repeater. _____
   _____
   _____
   _____

2. Define the term hub. _____
   _____
   _____
   _____

3. Define the term bridge. _____
   _____
   _____
   _____

4. Define the term switch. _____
   _____
   _____
   _____

5. Define the term router. _____
   _____
   _____
   _____

6. Define the term brouter. _____
   _____
   _____
   _____

7. Define the term gateway. _____
   _____
   _____
   _____

Review Questions

1. A gateway is a combination of networking hardware and software that connects two dissimilar networks.

   T _____ F _____

2. A brouter operates at Layers 2 and 3 of the OSI Model.

   T _____ F _____

3. In cut-through mode, a switch reads the whole data packet in its own RAM and verifies it for accuracy before transmitting it.

T _____ F _____

4. Hubs operate at Layer 1 of the OSI model.

T _____ F _____

5. What switching mode contributes to network congestion by forwarding network errors?

a. store and forward

b. cut-through

c. runt-forward

d. VLAN

6. Which bridging method is used on most Ethernet networks?

a. source route bridging

b. translational bridging

c. transparent bridging

d. brouter bridging

7. Switches provide separate channels for every device.

T _____ F _____

8. A router can connect dissimilar networks with different transmission speeds using a variety of protocols.

T _____ F _____

9. In which Layer of the OSI model does a router operate?

a. Layer 1

b. Layer 2

c. Layer 3

d. Layer 4

e. Layer 7

CHAPTER SEVEN

WANS AND REMOTE CONNECTIVITY

Labs included in this chapter

➤ Lab 7.1 Understanding WANs and LANs

➤ Lab 7.2 Establishing Remote Connectivity using Fiber-Optic Bridges

➤ Lab 7.3 Understanding WAN Transmission Methods

➤ Lab 7.4 Understanding T-Carriers

➤ Lab 7.5 Installing Point-to-Point Tunneling Protocol

➤ Lab 7.6 Installing Dial-Up Networking

LAB 7.1 UNDERSTANDING WANS AND LANS

Objective

The goal of this lab is to help you learn about the similarities and differences between WANs and LANs. After completing this lab, you will be able to:

➤ Identify characteristics of a WAN and a LAN

Materials Required

This lab will require the following:

➤ Pencil and paper

ACTIVITY

1. Define the term LAN. _____
   _____
   _____
   _____

2. Define the term WAN. _____
   _____
   _____
   _____

3. Identify three similarities between a LAN and a WAN. _____
   _____
   _____
   _____

4. List three differences between a LAN and a WAN. _____
   _____
   _____
   _____

5. Draw a LAN. Include computers, hubs, routers, and switches in your drawing.

6. Draw a WAN. Include computers, hubs, routers, and switches in your drawing.

Review Questions

1. You are more likely to have a WAN than a LAN in a home office.
   T _____ F _____

2. A WAN link is a connection between one site (or point) and another site (or point).
   T _____ F _____

3. Define the term point to point.

   _____

   _____

   _____

4. A WAN always takes the form of a bus topology.
   T _____ F _____

5. DeKalb Technical Institute, a postsecondary technical school, has campuses in Clarkston and Covington, Virginia; these cities are 35 miles apart. Would you use a WAN link or a LAN link to connect these two sites? _____

   _____

6. Explain your answer in Question 5. _____

   _____

   _____

   _____

7. Define the term dedicated line. _____

   _____

   _____

   _____

8. Joe owns a small company that sells computer equipment over the Internet. This company has its headquarters in Atlanta and one regional sales office in Miami. Would the company use a WAN link or a LAN link to connect these two sites? _____

   _____

9. Explain your answer to Question 8. _____
_____
_____
_____

10. Sally is testing five computers on an isolated network at her workplace. She is using the NetBEUI protocol for her test. Would she use a WAN link or a LAN link for her test?
_____

11. Explain your answer in Question 10. _____
_____
_____
_____

LAB 7.2 ESTABLISHING REMOTE CONNECTIVITY USING FIBER-OPTIC BRIDGES

Objectives

The goal of this lab is to help you gain an understanding of remote connectivity. You will connect two bridges to simulate a WAN. Each bridge will be connected to a hub; the hub will have other computers connected to it forming a LAN. After completing this lab, you will be able to:

➤ Simulate a WAN by installing a fiber-optic bridge that connects two separate LANs

➤ Understand WAN connectivity

Materials Required

This lab will require the following:

➤ Two working star topology networks, each with a 10/100-Mbps Ethernet hub

➤ A Windows NT Server 4.0 computer and at least one Windows NT Workstation 4.0 or Windows 95/98 client on each network

➤ A NIC for each computer, with a UTP cable connecting the NIC to the hub on one of the two star networks

➤ Two fiber-optic bridges with an AUI interface

➤ Two twisted-pair transceivers with an RJ-45 connection on one end and an AUI connection on the other end

➤ At least 6 feet of fiber-optic cable that is ready to connect to the bridges. The fiber-optic cable is actually made with a transmit and receive connection on each end.

➤ Two unshielded twisted-pair (UTP) cables

ACTIVITY

1. Connect one end of a UTP cable to one of the ports on one hub.

2. Connect the other end of the same UTP cable to the RJ-45 end of one of the transceivers.

3. Connect the AUI end of the transceiver used in Step 2 to the fiber-optic bridge.

4. Connect one end of the second UTP cable to one of the ports on the second hub.

5. Connect the other end of the second UTP cable to the RJ-45 end of the second transceiver.

6. Connect the AUI end of the second transceiver to the second fiber-optic bridge.

7. Connect one of the transmit and receive ends of the fiber-optic cable to one bridge.

8. Connect the other transmit and receive end of the same fiber-optic cable to the second bridge. Now the two star topology networks are connected via fiber, thereby simulating a WAN connection.

9. Log on to a Windows NT Workstation computer that is connected to one of the LANs.

10. Double-click the **Network Neighborhood** icon. Do you see an icon representing a computer on the other LAN?

_____

11. Log off the Windows NT workstation.

Review Questions

1. A WAN can be made of dissimilar LANs.
   T _____ F _____

2. FDDI is more expensive than UTP or STP cable.
   T _____ F _____

3. A LAN connects exactly two points.
   T _____ F _____

4. From a user's standpoint, there is no difference between using a LAN and a WAN.

   T _____ F _____

5. Discuss the effect that EMI and RFI have on FDDI.

   _____

   _____

   _____

6. What is the maximum speed of FDDI?

   a. 10 Mbps

   b. 100 Mbps

   c. 5 Kbps

   d. 100 MBps

LAB 7.3 UNDERSTANDING WAN TRANSMISSION METHODS

Objective

The goal of this lab is to help you learn more about the different ways of transmitting data over a WAN. After completing this lab, you will be able to:

➤ Identify the characteristics of different WAN transmission methods

Materials Required

This lab will require the following:

➤ Pencil and paper

➤ Internet access

ACTIVITY

1. Access the Internet Web site www.webopedia.com.

2. Search for the term PSTN. In your own words, record a definition for PSTN.

   _____

   _____

   _____

   _____

3. While the definition for PSTN is on the screen, click on the POTS link and record a definition in your own words. _____

   _____

   _____

   _____

4. Search for the term ISDN. In your own words, record a definition for the term ISDN. _____

_____

_____

_____

5. Search for the term xDSL. In your own words, record a definition for the term xDSL. _____

_____

_____

_____

6. While the definition for xDSL is on the screen, click ADSL and then SDSL, and compare these xDSL categories.

_____

_____

_____

7

Review Questions

1. Define the term modem. _____

_____

_____

_____

2. Which of the following is true of PSTN? Choose all that apply.
   a. It is sometimes called "Plain Old Telephone Service" or "POTS."
   b. It was originally developed to handle analog transmission.
   c. A dial-up connection uses a PSTN to access a remote computer via a modem.
   d. The current maximum speed is 56 Kbps.

3. A POP is a location where two telephone systems meet.
   T _____ F _____

4. All ISDN connections have two channels.
   T _____ F _____

5. BRI uses two "B" channels and one "D" channel.
   T _____ F _____

6. A "B" channel carries data.
   T _____ F _____

7. A "D" channel carries voice, video, and audio transmissions.
   T _____ F _____

8. DSL uses data modulation to achieve high throughput over telephone lines.
   T _____ F _____

LAB 7.4 UNDERSTANDING T-CARRIERS

Objectives

The goal of this lab is to help you become conversant in T-carrier terminology. In order to complete this lab, you will be required to visit a local business, school, or other organization that has a WAN. After completing this lab, you will be able to:

➤ Define terms related to T-carrier technology

➤ Identify WAN hardware components

Materials Required

In this lab, you will need the following:

➤ Someone willing to give you a tour of a WAN

➤ Pencil and paper

ACTIVITY

1. Contact a business, school, government office, or other site and ask to interview the person in charge of the organization's WAN. Explain that your purpose is purely educational and that you desire to learn more about WANs. Also, explain that you will need to take notes.

2. Record the name of the organization: _____

_____

3. Make the visit and observe the WAN.

4. Does the site use a T1, T2, T3, or T4 line? _____

_____

5. On a separate piece of paper, draw the site's WAN topology using boxes to represent WAN components. Draw lines to connect the components.

6. Label the components using "M" for a multiplexer, "CSU" for a channel service unit, "DSU" for a data service unit, "P" for a PBX or a phone system, "R" for a router, and an "L" for a LAN.

7. Thank the person you interviewed.

8. Follow up with a letter of thanks.

Review Questions

1. A CSU converts the digital signal used by bridges and routers into the digital signal sent over the T-carrier cabling.

   T _____ F _____

2. A multiplexer combines multiple data or voice signals into one line.

   T _____ F _____

3. A DSU provides termination for the digital signal and handles error correction and line monitoring.

   T _____ F _____

4. What is the maximum distance for a T1 line using STP?

   a. 600 meters

   b. 6000 meters

   c. 6000 feet

   d. 6 kilometers

   e. 100 meters

5. A fractional T1 line can be leased in multiples of 64 Kbps.

   T _____ F _____

6. Define the term multiplexer. _____

   _____

   _____

   _____

7. How many channels does a T1 line have?

   a. 1

   b. 2

   c. 12

   d. 24

   e. 672

8. What is the maximum throughput of a T3 connection?

   a. 64 Kbps

   b. 1.544 Mbps

   c. 672 Mbps

   d. 45 Mbps

   e. 275 Mbps

7

LAB 7.5 INSTALLING POINT-TO-POINT TUNNELING PROTOCOL

Objectives

The goal of this lab is to help you learn how to install the Point-to-Point Tunneling Protocol (PPTP). PPTP requires the use of Remote Access Services (RAS); so, RAS will be installed too. After completing this lab, you will be able to:

➤ Install PPTP

➤ Install RAS

Materials Required

This lab will require the following:

➤ A Windows NT Server 4.0 computer that only has TCP/IP as the installed protocol

➤ A modem connected to the COM2 serial port of the Windows NT 4 Server computer

ACTIVITY

1. Log on as an administrator. The Windows desktop appears.

2. Right-click the **Network Neighborhood** icon.

3. Click **Properties**. The Network dialog box appears.

4. Click **Protocols**. The list of installed protocols appears in the Network Protocols list.

5. Click **Add**. The Select Network Protocol dialog box appears.

6. Click **Point to Point Tunneling Protocol** in the Network Protocol list.

7. Click **OK**. The Windows NT Setup dialog box appears with the drive letter of the CD-ROM and the path to the I386 folder.

8. Make sure the drive letter is correct.

9. Insert the Windows NT 4.0 Server installation CD into the CD-ROM drive.

10. Click **Continue**. The Windows NT Setup program copies files to the hard disk drive. The PPTP Configuration dialog box appears.

11. Make sure **1** is selected in the Number of Virtual Private Connections scroll box.

12. Click **OK**. The Setup Message dialog box appears, indicating that Remote Access Services (RAS) will be installed.

13. Click **OK**. The Setup program copies files to the hard disk drive. The Add RAS Device dialog box appears.

14. Click **OK**. The Remote Access Setup dialog box appears.

15. Click **Continue**. The RAS Server TCP/IP Configuration dialog box appears, similar to the one in Figure 7-1. The TCP/IP settings are stored in the Registry on the hard disk drive.

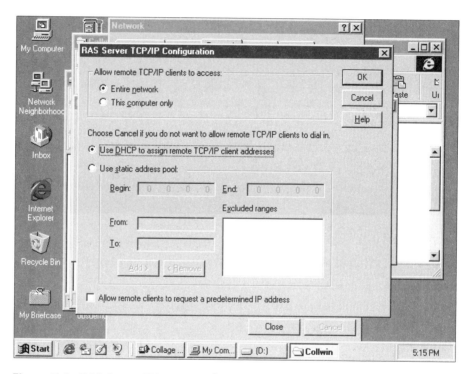

Figure 7-1 RAS Server TCP/IP Configuration dialog box.

16. Click **OK.** The Setup Message dialog box appears, indicating RAS has been successfully installed.

17. Click **OK**. An entry for Point to Point Tunneling Protocol appears in the Network Protocol list.

18. Click **Close**. The Network Settings Change dialog box appears.

19. Click **Yes** to restart the computer. PPTP and RAS are now installed, making it possible for a Windows NT Workstation 4.0 computer or a Windows 95 or Windows 98 computer to access this server. These computers must have Dial-Up Networking installed in order to dial the Windows NT 4.0 server.

Review Questions

1. What is the purpose of Dial-Up Networking? _____

_____

_____

_____

2. A modem is never used when dialing an ISP.

   T _____ F _____

3. Differentiate between SLIP and PPP. _____

_____

_____

_____

4. Define the term synchronous. _____

_____

_____

_____

5. Define the term asynchronous. _____

_____

_____

_____

6. SLIP requires you to specify the IP addresses for both the client and server.

   T _____ F _____

7. PPTP allows you to obtain the IP address automatically for a client and server.

   T _____ F _____

LAB NOTES

PPTP is sometimes referred to as PPP.

A Windows NT 4.0 Server can handle up to 256 incoming connections; in PPTP terms, these are virtual private connections (VPCs).

LAB 7.6 INSTALLING DIAL-UP NETWORKING

Objectives

The goal of this lab is to help you learn how to install Dial-Up Networking (DUN). You will also install RAS on the workstation. After completing this lab, you will be able to:

➤ Install DUN

➤ Create a Phone Book entry for DUN

➤ Simulate remote connectivity by connecting two Windows NT 4.0 computers together using DUN over a null-modem cable

Materials Required

This lab will require the following:

➤ A Windows NT Workstation 4.0 computer with TCP/IP as the only installed protocol

➤ A Windows NT Workstation 4.0 computer that has RAS installed, with TCP/IP as the only installed protocol

➤ The Windows NT Workstation 4.0 installation CD

➤ A null-modem cable connected to the COM2 serial port of the Windows NT 4.0 Workstation computer

7

ACTIVITY

1. Log on as an administrator.

2. Double-click **My Computer**, then double-click the Dial-Up Networking icon. The Dial-Up Networking dialog box appears. Because this is the first time you have attempted to use DUN, you are prompted to install it first.

3. Click **Install**. The Files Needed dialog box appears.

4. Insert the installation CD into the CD-ROM drive and verify the path.

5. Click **OK**.

6. The Remote Access Service Setup dialog box appears with a progress bar indicating RAS is being installed. DUN is installed. Next, the Remote Access Setup dialog box appears asking you to add an RAS capable device.

7. Click **Yes**. The Install New Modem dialog box appears.

8. Check **Don't detect my modem; I will select it from a list** and click **Next**. After a pause (possibly as long as a few minutes), a list of modem manufacturers and model types appears.

9. Click **(Standard Modem Types)** in the manufacturer's list, click **Dial-Up Network Serial Cable between 2 PCs** and click **Next**. A list of ports appears.

10. Click **COM2** and click **Next**. The Location Information dialog box appears. Enter **770** in the Area Code text box and click **Next**. You see a message indicating that the modem is installed.

11. Click **Finish**. The Add RAS Device dialog box appears.

12. Click **OK**. The Remote Access Setup dialog box appears with COM2 as the port and Dial-Up network serial cable between 2 PCs as the device.

13. Click **Continue**. The Dial-Up Networking dialog box appears, prompting you to restart the computer.

14. Click **Restart**.

15. After the computer restarts, log on as an administrator.

16. Double-click **My Computer** and then double-click the **Dial-Up Networking** icon. The Dial-Up Networking dialog box appears, prompting you to add a phonebook entry.

17. Click **OK**. The New Phonebook Entry Wizard dialog box appears.

18. In the **Name the new phonebook entry**, type **DialNT** and click **Next**. The Server dialog box appears.

19. Click **Next**. The Phone Number dialog box appears.

20. Click **Next**. The Phone Number Entry Wizard dialog box appears, indicating that DialNT was added.

21. Click **Finish** to save the phonebook entry. The dial-up network dialog box appears.

22. Connect the null-modem cable to the two computers.

23. You can now dial out to another computer running RAS.

Review Questions

1. SLIP can only support TCP/IP.
   T _____ F _____

2. PPP can support TCP/IP, NWLink, and NetBEUI.
   T _____ F _____

3. Define RAS. _____
   _____
   _____
   _____

LAB NOTES

A null modem cable is a serial cable that is used to simulate a modem. You can purchase one at an electronics store.

NETWORK OPERATING SYSTEMS AND WINDOWS NT-BASED NETWORKING

Labs included in this chapter

➤ Lab 8.1 Converting from a FAT File System to an NTFS File System

➤ Lab 8.2 Establishing a One-way Trust Relationship

➤ Lab 8.3 Promoting a BDC to a PDC

➤ Lab 8.4 Understanding Groups

➤ Lab 8.5 Sharing Folders and Setting Permissions on an NTFS File System

Lab 8.1 Converting from a FAT File System to an NTFS File System

Objectives

The goal of this lab is to help you learn how to convert a FAT file system to NTFS. After completing this lab, you will be able to:

➤ Describe the purpose of the Windows NT convert command

➤ Convert a file system from FAT to NTFS

Materials Required

This lab will require the following:

➤ A computer running Windows NT Server 4.0 or Windows NT Workstation 4.0, with drive D formatted as FAT

➤ Windows NT Server 4.0 or Windows NT Workstation 4.0 loaded on the drive D partition

Activity

1. Log on as an administrator.

2. Double-click the **My Computer** icon. The My Computer window opens, displaying the drives and folders on your computer.

3. Right-click the **D: drive** icon.

4. Click **Properties**. The D: Properties dialog box opens.

5. Verify that the file system type is FAT.

6. Click **Start**, point to **Programs**, and then click **Command Prompt**. The Command Prompt window opens.

7. Type **convert /?** to open the online Help page explaining the convert command.

8. Read the Help page. What is the purpose of the convert command?

_____

_____

9. Type **convert d: /fs:ntfs /v** at the command prompt. A message appears indicating that the convert utility cannot begin the conversion because it cannot gain access to the D: drive. It prompts you to reschedule the conversion, so that it occurs after you restart the system.

10. Press **Y** to reschedule the conversion.

11. Type **exit** at the command prompt. The Command Prompt window closes.

12. Click **Start**, click **Shutdown**, and click **Restart** and then click **Yes** to restart the computer. During the boot sequence, the conversion occurs.

13. Repeat Steps 1 through 4.

14. Record the file system type. _____

_____

Review Questions

1. HPFS is designed for the OS/2 operating system.
   T _____ F _____

2. You can convert NTFS to FAT.
   T _____ F _____

3. Define the term file system. _____

_____

_____

_____

4. List the file systems that Windows NT Server supports: _____

_____

_____

_____

5. An NTFS file system cannot exceed 4 GB.
   T _____ F _____

6. What is the maximum number of characters in an NTFS filename?
   a. 8
   b. 11
   c. 16
   d. 255
   e. 256

7. The FAT file system can use NTFS security.
   T _____ F _____

8. What is the difference between FAT and FAT32? _____

_____

_____

_____

9. What is the difference between FAT and NTFS? _____

_____

_____

_____

8

LAB 8.2 ESTABLISHING A ONE-WAY TRUST RELATIONSHIP

Objective

The goal of this lab is to help you understand how a one-way trust is implemented. After completing this lab, you will be able to:

➤ Establish a one-way trust relationship

Materials Required

This lab will require the following:

➤ Two domains, one named Domain_1 and one named Domain_2

➤ One Windows NT Server computer acting as PDC in Domain_1

➤ One Windows NT Server computer acting as PDC in Domain_2

ACTIVITY

1. Log on to the Domain_1 PDC as an administrator.

2. Click **Start**, point to **Programs**, point to **Administrative Tools (Common)**, and then click **User Manager for Domains**. The User Manager window opens.

3. Click **Policies** and then click **Trust Relationships**. The Trust Relationships dialog box opens, as in Figure 8-1.

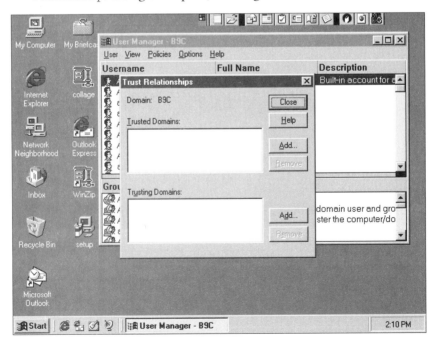

Figure 8-1 Trust Relationships dialog box

4. In the Trusting Domains portion of the dialog box, click **Add**. The Add Trusting Domain dialog box opens.

5. In the Trusting Domain text box, type **Domain_2**, and then click **OK**. The domain is added to the list of trusting domains. You have completed the first part of the one-way trust relationship.

6. Log on to the PDC that is in Domain_2.

7. Repeat Steps 2 and 3.

8. In the Trusted Domain dialog box, click **Add**. The Add Trusted Domain dialog box opens.

9. In the Trusted Domain part of the text box, type **Domain_1** and then click **OK**. After a few seconds, the User Manager for Domains dialog box opens indicating the trust relationship was successfully established, and the domain is added to the list of trusted domains. You have completed the last part of the one-way trust relationship.

10. Exit User Manager on both computers and log off.

Review Questions

1. In trust relationships, the domain that grants access to its resources is known as the trusted domain.

   T _____ F _____

2. In trust relationships, the domain that accesses resources is known as the trusting domain.

   T _____ F _____

3. Define the term trust relationship. _____

   _____

   _____

4. Define the term complete trust domain model. _____

   _____

   _____

5. A single Windows NT domain can support up to 2,600 users.

   T _____ F _____

6. A master domain model can support a maximum of 30,000 users.

   T _____ F _____

7. With four domains, how many trust relationships must be configured in a complete trust domain model?

    a. 4

    b. 16

    c. 3

    d. 12

    e. 2

LAB 8.3 PROMOTING A BDC TO A PDC

Objective

The goal of this lab is to help you learn more about domain controllers. After completing this lab, you will be able to:

➤ Promote a BDC to a PDC

Materials Required

This lab will require the following:

➤ Two computers with Windows NT Server installed

➤ One computer installed as the PDC

➤ The other computer installed as the BDC

ACTIVITY

1. Log on to the PDC as an administrator.

2. Click **Start**, point to **Programs**, point to **Administrative Tools (Common),** and then click **Server Manager**. The Server Manager window opens.

3. Scroll until you find Windows NT 4.0 Backup in the Type column, and then click on the icon representing the BDC.

4. Click **Computer**.

5. Click **Promote to Primary Domain Controller**. The Server Manager dialog box opens, indicating that this may take a few minutes. A clock appears in the left-hand side of this dialog box with a second hand that moves to indicate the change is occurring. Once complete, the old BDC is the PDC, and the old PDC is the BDC.

6. To reverse the roles, repeat Steps 1 through 5.

Review Questions

1. A domain can have two PDCs.

   T _____ F _____

2. Define the term domain. _____

   _____

   _____

   _____

3. What is the purpose of a BDC? _____

   _____

   _____

   _____

4. What is the difference between a member server and a domain controller?

   _____

   _____

   _____

5. A workstation can be a domain controller.

   T _____ F _____

6. A member server can be promoted to a BDC.

   T _____ F _____

7. A server in a Windows NT domain must be either a PDC, a BDC, or a member server.

   T _____ F _____

8

LAB 8.4 UNDERSTANDING GROUPS

Objectives

The goal of this lab is to help you understand Windows NT groups. After completing this lab, you will be able to:

➤ Create a user

➤ Create a local group

➤ Create a global group

➤ Add a user to a global group

➤ Add a global group to a local group

Materials Required

In this lab, you will need the following:

➤ One Windows NT Server 4.0 computer installed as a PDC in Domain_A

➤ One Windows NT Workstation computer in Domain_A

ACTIVITY

1. Log on to the PDC as an administrator.

2. Click **Start**, point to **Programs**, point to **Administrative Tools (Common)**, and then click **User Manager for Domains**. The User Manager window opens.

3. Click **User** and then click **New User**. The New User dialog box opens.

4. In the Username text box, type your name.

5. Click **Add**. The new user is added.

6. Click **Close**.

7. Click **User**, then click **New Global Group**. The New Global Group dialog box opens. One pane shows the group members, and the other shows nonmembers.

8. In the Group Name box, type **GG_1**.

9. In the Not Member scroll box, click the username you created in Step 4.

10. Click **Add**. The user is added to the Members list.

11. Click **OK**. The global group is added to the domain. At this point, you have added the user to the global group.

12. Now, log on to the workstation as an administrator.

13. Click **Start**, point to **Programs**, point to **Administrative Tools (Common)**, and then click **User Manager**. The User Manager window opens. Notice there is no User Manager for Domains on the workstation.

14. Click **User**, and then click **New Local Group**. The New Local Group dialog box opens.

15. In the Group Name text box, type **LG_1**.

16. Click **Add**. The Add Users and Group dialog box opens.

17. In the List Names From box, click **Domain_1**.

18. Click **GG_1**.

19. To see the members of GG_1, click **Members**. The Global Group Membership dialog box opens.

20. Record the members. _____

_____

21. Click **Cancel**.

22. Click **Add** to add GG_1 to the local group. The global group now appears in the Add Names box.

23. Click **OK** twice. You have finished adding the global group in the domain to the local group on the workstation.

Review Questions

1. What is the purpose of a group? _____

_____

_____

2. It is possible to add groups to users in Windows NT.
   T _____ F _____

3. Every new user is a member of the "Everyone" group.
   T _____ F _____

4. A username may contain a maximum of six characters.
   T _____ F _____

5. Which of the following are valid passwords? Choose all that apply.
   a. FUN
   b. fun
   c. thisismypassword
   d. cars+trucks
   e. x

6. Users can be members of multiple groups.
   T _____ F _____

7. A local group contains resources from multiple domains.
   T _____ F _____

LAB NOTES

Microsoft suggests the following procedure: place users in global groups; then place global groups into local groups; then assign permissions to the local group where the resource exists.

LAB 8.5 SHARING FOLDERS AND SETTING PERMISSIONS ON AN NTFS FILE SYSTEM

Objectives

The intent of this lab is to help you understand how to share folders and set permissions in Windows NT 4. After completing this lab, you will be able to:

➤ Share folders

➤ Understand NTFS share permissions

Materials Required

In this lab, you will need the following:

➤ Completion of Lab 8.4

➤ One Windows NT Server 4.0 computer installed as the PDC in Domain_A

➤ One Windows NT Workstation 4.0 computer named WSA in Domain_A

➤ Drive D on the Windows NT Workstation formatted as NTFS

ACTIVITY

1. Log on to the Windows NT Workstation as an administrator.

2. Double-click the **My Computer** icon. The My Computer window opens.

3. Double-click the **D: drive** icon. The D: Properties dialog box opens.

4. Click **File**, point to **New**, and then click **Folder**. A new folder is created and you are prompted to enter a folder name.

5. Name the folder **FolderR**.

6. Right-click the icon for **FolderR** and then click **Sharing**. The Properties window for FolderR opens.

7. Click **Shared As**. The name of the folder appears in the Share Name box. Do not change the share name.

8. Click **Permissions**. The Access Through Share Permissions dialog box opens.

9. Record the name of the group that appears by default.

_____

10. Record the permissions for the group that appears by default.

_____

11. Remove the group that appears by clicking it and then clicking **Remove**.

12. Click **Add**. The Add Users and Groups dialog box opens.

13. In the List Names From scroll box, select **WSA**. The list of groups on the workstation is displayed in the Names box.

14. Select **LG_1** and click **Add**. The entry appears in the Add Names box.

15. Click **Read** in the Type of Access scroll box.

16. Record the other types of access. _____

_____

17. Click **OK**. The local group, LG_1, appears in the Names list of the Access Through Share Permissions dialog box.

18. Click **OK** twice. At this point, you have added the local group, LG_1, with read access to FolderR. The user you created in Lab 8.4 has read access to the folder.

19. In order to verify that the user created in Lab 8.4 only has read access to FolderR, log off as administrator and then log on as the user you created in Step 4 of Lab 8.4. After you log on as this user, the Windows NT desktop appears.

20. Double-click **Network Neighborhood**. The Network Neighborhood window opens, displaying a list of computers.

21. Double-click the **WSA** icon. The WSA window opens.

22. Double-click on the **FolderR** folder. The FolderR window opens.

23. Click **File**, point to **New**, and then click **Folder**.

24. What message appears? _____

_____

25. Why did this message appear? _____

_____

26. In order to learn about the Full Control share permission, repeat this lab and create a folder named FolderF. Give the local group LG_1 Full Control as the type of access to FolderF.

27. Log on as the user you created in Step 4 of Lab 8.4. The Windows NT desktop appears.

28. Attempt to open FolderF and create another folder within it. Can you?

_____

29. In order to learn about the No Access share permission, repeat this lab and create a folder named FolderN. Give the local group LG_1 Full Control as the type of access to FolderN.

30. Log on as the user you created in Step 4 of Lab 8.4. The Windows NT desktop appears.

31. Attempt to open FolderN and create another folder within it. Can you?

_____

Review Questions

1. What is the purpose of permissions?_____

_____

_____

_____

2. What will the Read permission allow?_____

_____

_____

_____

3. The Change permission allows a user to read, delete, and modify files.
   T _____ F _____

4. What is the difference between the No Access and the Full Control permission? _____

_____

5. The Full Control permission allows users to read and modify a file.
   T _____ F _____

6. You can assign permissions to groups as well as users.
   T _____ F _____

7. What are the default permissions for a shared folder? _____

_____

_____

8. What does the hand graphic below a folder indicate?_____

_____

9. A protocol is never used when connecting to an ISP.
   T _____ F _____

NetWare-based Networking

Labs included in this chapter

➤ Lab 9.1 Starting and Shutting Down a Novell NetWare 4.11 Server

➤ Lab 9.2 Understanding NetWare Volumes

➤ Lab 9.3 Understanding Drive Mappings

➤ Lab 9.4 Understanding NDS Objects

➤ Lab 9.5 Understanding NDS Contexts

LAB 9.1 STARTING AND SHUTTING DOWN A NOVELL NETWARE 4.11 SERVER

Objectives

The goal of this lab is to help you learn how to start and stop the Novell NetWare Server operating system. After completing this lab, you will be able to:

➤ Start up a Novell NetWare 4.11 server

➤ Shut down a Novell NetWare 4.11 server

➤ Understand what occurs on a client when a server is shut down

➤ Understand the purpose of the kernel

Materials Required

This lab will require the following:

➤ A computer named ONE with Novell NetWare 4.11 Server installed in C:\NWSERVER

➤ A computer with Windows 95 and the Novell Client 32 software installed

➤ A functioning connection between the server and the client computer

ACTIVITY

1. Boot the Novell NetWare 4.11 Server computer.

2. At the C:\> prompt, type **CD \NWSERVER** and press **Enter**. The prompt changes to C:\NWSERVER>.

3. At the C:\NWSERVER> prompt, type **SERVER** and press **Enter**. The Novell NetWare Server kernel, SERVER.EXE, loads into the computer's RAM. The server prompt changes to ONE:, indicating that the server (named ONE) is up and running.

4. Now you can attempt to access the server from the Windows 95 client computer. At the client computer, click **Start**, point to **Programs**, point to **Novell**, and then click **NetWare Login**. The Novell NetWare Login window opens.

5. Click the **Login** tab (if necessary), click the **Name** text box, type **ADMIN**, click the **Password** text box and then type the password for the client computer.

6. Click **OK**. The Login Results window opens, indicating that you logged in successfully. Now that you are logged in to the client computer, you will attempt to shut down the server, and observe the effect on the client computer.

7. Go back to the server and verify that the ONE: prompt is still displayed.

8. Type **DOWN** and press **Enter**. The Novell NetWare 4.11 Server operating system is unloaded from RAM.

9. Look at the screen on the Windows 95 client computer. What message do you see? _____
   _____

10. Click **Close** to close the message on the client computer.

11. Repeat the necessary steps to start the Novell NetWare 4.11 server again.

12. To login from the Windows 95 client computer, repeat Steps 4 through 6.

Review Questions

1. Define the term kernel. _____
   _____
   _____
   _____

2. What command starts the Novell Server network operating system?
   a. KERNEL.EXE
   b. NOS.EXE
   c. SERVER.EXE
   d. UP.EXE
   e. SERVER.COM

3. What DOS file automatically starts a Novell server?
   a. AUTOEXEC.EXE
   b. CONFIG.SYS
   c. SERVER.EXE
   d. AUTOEXEC.BAT
   e. NLM

4. A Novell NetWare 4.11 server has a graphical interface for administering NDS.
   T _____ F _____

5. What is the name of the graphical interface that runs on a Novell NetWare 5.0 server?
   a. SERVER.EXE
   b. MONITOR
   c. ConsoleOne
   d. AUTOEXEC.BAT

9

6. On a Novell NetWare 4.11 server, you can manage the NetWare File System.

   T _____ F _____

7. In order to view NLMs currently loaded on a Novell NetWare 4.11 server, you run the modules command.

   T _____ F _____

8. Define the term NLM. _____

   _____

   _____

   _____

9. NLMs can be executed at a workstation.

   T _____ F _____

LAB 9.2 UNDERSTANDING NETWARE VOLUMES

Objectives

The goal of this lab is to help you understand Novell NetWare volumes. After completing this lab, you will be able to:

➤ Create a NetWare partition from free space on a disk

➤ Create a NetWare volume from the partition

➤ View volume properties such as compression and block suballocation

Materials Required

This lab will require the following:

➤ A computer named NW5_5 running Novell NetWare 5.0 Server

➤ At least 500 MB of free disk space on the Novell NetWare 5.0 Server computer's hard disk

➤ The NDS organization named NW5_O, with the Admin user in this container

ACTIVITY

1. At the Novell NetWare 5.0 Server console, press **Alt+Esc**. You see the server console, NW5:.

2. Type **nwconfig** and press **Enter**.

3. Use the arrow keys to select **Standard Disk Options**, and press **Enter**. The Available Disk Options dialog box opens.

4. Use the arrow keys to select **Modify disk partitions and Hot Fix**, and press **Enter**. A table showing the disk partitions and their sizes appears.

5. Use the arrow keys to select **Create NetWare disk partition**, and press **Enter**. The Disk Partition Information dialog box opens.

6. In this step, you need to be familiar with the parts of a partition. A partition is made of two parts. The area where data is actually stored is known as the data area. Another area of the disk, known as the redirection area or the "hot fix," is reserved for redirecting bad disk blocks. The default size for the "hot fix" depends upon the partition size but usually takes up between 5% and 10% of the total partition size. In the Partition size text box, type **500** and press **Enter**. The Data Area changes to a slightly smaller amount, and the redirection area increases. For example, the data area might decrease to 497 MB, while the redirection area increases by the difference, or 3 MB.

7. Press **F10** to save your changes. The Create NetWare Partition? dialog box opens.

8. Use the arrow keys to select **Yes**, and then press **Enter**. Novell adds the new partition.

9. Press the **Esc** key. The Available Disk Options window reappears.

10. Use the arrow keys to select **NetWare Volume Options**, and then press **Enter**. The volume names and sizes appear.

11. Note what volume names and sizes appear. _____

    _____

12. Now you can create a new volume. The first step in this process is to determine the amount of free space available. Press the **Ins** key. The Volume Disk Segment List dialog box appears.

13. Record the amount of free space. _____

    _____

14. Next, you will make a volume assignment from the free space. Use the arrow keys to select **(free space)**, and press **Enter**. The What would you like to do with this free segment? dialog box opens.

15. Use the arrow keys to select **Make this segment a new volume**, and then press **Enter**. The Disk segment parameters dialog box opens.

16. In the Disk segment volume name text box, type **APPS2** and press **Enter**. The cursor highlights the Disk segment size text box. Do not change the size.

17. Press **F10**. The new volume is added. The Volume Disk Segment List reappears.

18. Press **Esc** twice. The Save volume changes? dialog box opens.

9

19. Use the arrow keys to select **Yes**, and then press **Enter**. The Directory Services Login/Authentication dialog box opens.

20. In the Administrator name text box, type **.CN=Admin.O=NW5_5** and then press **Enter**. In the Password text box, type the password for the Admin user and then press **Enter**. The For your information dialog box opens indicating that the volume has been installed.

21. Press **Enter** to continue. The Select an action dialog box opens.

22. Use the arrow keys to select **Mount all volumes**, and then press **Enter**. The Available Disk Options window reappears.

23. Press **Esc** twice. The Exit nwconfig? dialog box opens.

24. Use the arrow keys to select **Yes**, and then press **Enter**. The NW5_5 server prompt appears. You have added a NetWare partition created from free space on the server's hard disk, and you have added a volume within that NetWare partition. Next, you will verify the volume's properties.

25. At the server console NW5_5 prompt, type **nwconfig** and press **Enter**.

26. Use the arrow keys to select **Standard Disk Options**, and then press **Enter**. The Available Disk Options screen opens.

27. Use the arrow keys to select **NetWare Volume Options**, and then press **Enter**. The volume names and sizes appear.

28. Use the arrow keys to select the volume named **APPS2**, which you created earlier in this lab, and then press **Enter**. The Volume information for APPS2 appears.

29. What is the volume's status? _____

_____

30. Is file compression turned on or off? _____

_____

31. Is block suballocation turned on or off? _____

_____

32. Press **Esc** four times. The Exit nwconfig? dialog box opens.

33. Use the arrow keys to select **Yes**, and then press **Enter**. The **NW5_5** server prompt appears.

Review Questions

1. Define the term volume. _____

_____

_____

_____

2. What is the name of NetWare's default volume?

 a. DATA

 b. SYSTEM

 c. SYS

 d. APPS

3. Creating a separate volume for data files is more secure than placing all the data and system files in the same volume.

 T _____ F _____

4. Compression is recommended for extremely large files.

 T _____ F _____

5. What is the purpose of block suballocation? _____

_____

_____

_____

6. Block suballocation is not enabled by default.

 T _____ F _____

7. The amount of space saved with compression varies with each file.

 T _____ F _____

8. NetWare uses volumes to organize files and directories on a client.

 T _____ F _____

9

 The steps in this lab can also be completed on a Novell NetWare 4.11 server.

 A volume must be mounted in order to be used by client computers. A volume will have a status of either mounted or unmounted.

LAB 9.3 UNDERSTANDING DRIVE MAPPINGS

Objectives

The goal of this lab is to help you learn more about Novell NetWare drive mappings. After completing this lab, you will be able to:

➤ Create a drive mapping

➤ Delete a drive mapping

Materials Required

This lab will require the following:

➤ Knowledge of the md and dir DOS commands

➤ Completion of Lab 9.2

➤ A computer named NW5_5 running Novell NetWare 5.0 Server

➤ A computer running Windows 95/98 and the Novell Client 32 software

➤ A computer with Internet access

➤ A functioning network connection between the two computers

ACTIVITY

1. Go to the computer with Internet access. Go to *www.webopedia.com* and search for "map".

2. Define the term map. _____

   _____

3. Go to the Windows 95/98 client computer and log on to the Novell NetWare 5.0 Server computer as Admin.

4. Click **Start**, point to **Programs** and then click **MS-DOS Prompt**. The MS-DOS Prompt window opens.

5. At the prompt, type **map** and then press **Enter** to display the current drive mappings.

6. Record the current mappings. _____

   _____

   _____

   _____

7. Type **map H:= NW5_5\APPS2:** and then press **Enter** to set a drive mapping. The new drive mapping returns.

8. Type **map** and then press **Enter** to display the new drive mapping. You see a list of drive mappings.

9. Type **H:** and then press **Enter** to change to the newly mapped drive. The new prompt H:\APPS2 appears.

10. Type **dir** and then press **Enter**. A list of the current files and directories on this drive appears.

11. Are there any files or folders on this drive? _____

    _____

12. Type **md fun** and then press **Enter** to create a new directory. The prompt returns.

13. Type **map next nw5_5\apps2:\fun** and then press **Enter** to create a drive mapping to this newly created directory.

14. Type **map** and then press **Enter** to display the current drive mappings. You see the list of drive mappings.

15. Record the drive letter mapped to the fun directory.

16. Type **map del H:** and then press **Enter** to delete the H: mapped drive. A message appears indicating that the drive mapping has been deleted.

17. Type **exit** and then press **Enter** to exit the MS-DOS Prompt window. The Windows desktop appears.

 A workstation can accommodate no more than 26 drive mappings.

 A drive mapping is a reference to a directory stored on a Novell NetWare volume.

Review Questions

1. What is the purpose of the map command? _____
   _____
   _____
   _____

2. A drive letter is mapped to a Novell NetWare 5.0 volume.
   T _____ F _____

3. You can delete a drive mapping.
   T _____ F _____

4. Drive mappings operate within NDS, not within the NetWare File System.
   T _____ F _____

5. There can be up to 26 mapped drives on a workstation.
   T _____ F _____

6. You execute the map command while at a Novell NetWare 5.0 Server.
   T _____ F _____

Lab 9.4 Understanding NDS Objects

Objective

The intent of this lab is to help you understand how to create NDS objects. After completing this lab, you will be able to:

➤ Create Organizational Unit objects

➤ Create User objects

➤ Create Group objects

➤ Add User objects to Group objects

➤ Make trustee assignments

Materials Required

In this lab, you will need the following:

➤ A computer named NW5_5 running Novell NetWare 5.0 Server

➤ An NDS organization named NW5_O

➤ A computer running Windows 95/98 and the Novell Client 32 software

➤ A functioning network connection between the two computers

Activity

1. Go to the Windows 95/98 client computer and log on to the Novell NetWare 5.0 Server as Admin.

2. Double-click **Network Neighborhood**. The Network Neighborhood window opens.

3. Double-click the **NW5_5** server icon. The NW5_5 window opens, displaying a list of folders that exist on the server. The SYS folder represents the **SYS** volume.

4. Double-click the **SYS** folder. The SYS on NW5_5 window opens, displaying other folders within the SYS folder.

5. Double-click the **Public** folder. The Public folder opens; it contains a Win32 folder.

6. Double-click the **Win32** folder. The Win32 folder opens; it contains a program named Nwadmn32.

7. Double-click the program **Nwadmn32**. NetWare Administrator opens, displaying an NDS tree .

8. Click **NW5_O** and then click **Object**. The New Object dialog box opens.

9. Click **Organization Unit** (you may have to scroll first) and then click **OK**. The Create Organizational Unit dialog box opens.

10. In the Organizational Unit name text box, type **SALES** and click **Create**. The new object is added to the tree.

11. Click **SALES**, click **Object**, click **Create**, and then click the **User** object.

12. Click **OK**. The Create User window opens.

13. In the Login name text box, type **MICKI**.

14. Press **Tab** to move the cursor to the Last name text box. Type **Meadors** and click **Create**. The new user named **MICKI** is created. The NDS tree reappears with SALES highlighted.

15. Click **Object**, click **Create,** scroll the **New Object** dialog box, click the **Group** object, and then click **OK**. The Create Group window opens.

16. In the Group name text box, type **GROUP_A**, and then click **Create**. The new group is added to SALES. Now that you've created a group, you can add a user to it.

17. Double-click **GROUP_A**. The **Group: Group_A** Properties dialog box appears.

18. Click **Members**.

19. Record the list of group members. _____
_____

20. Click **Add**. The Select Object dialog box opens.

21. Click **MICKI** and then click **OK**. The user is added to the Group members list.

22. Click **OK**. You return to the NDS tree.

23. To verify that the user is a member of the group, double-click **MICKI**. The **Users: MICKI** Properties dialog box appears.

24. Click **Group Membership**. A list of groups to which the user belongs appears.

25. Note what groups does the user MICKI belong to? _____
_____

26. Click **Cancel** to return to the NDS tree. Now you will make a trustee assignment. A trustee is a user object that has certain rights to perform activities. For example, if a user is given the Create right to a container, the user can create objects within that container; the user is then considered a trustee of that container.

9

27. Right-click **SALES**, click **Trustees of this object**. The **Trustees of SALES** dialog box opens.

28. Click **Add Trustee…**. The Select Object dialog box opens.

29. In the **Browse context** dialog box, click **SALES**. MICKI is included in the **Available objects** list. Click **MICKI** and then click **OK**. The user MICKI appears in the Trustees list. A list of default object rights also appears.

30. What default object rights appear in the list? _____
_____

31. Select the **Supervisor**, **Create**, **Delete**, and **Rename** check boxes, and then click **OK**. You return to the NDS tree.

32. Log on from the client computer as MICKI.

33. Following the steps in this lab, try to add a user object to the SALES container.

34. Can you? _____
_____

35. Log out as user MICKI.

Review Questions

1. Define the term NDS. _____
_____
_____
_____

2. What is the purpose of an organizational unit? _____
_____
_____
_____

3. What do you call the object at the top of the NDS tree?
   a. root
   b. [Root]
   c. \
   d. /
   e. container

4. A user is an example of a container object.
   T _____ F _____

5. An organizational unit is an example of a leaf object.
   T _____ F _____

6. In Novell NetWare 4.11, the Bindery is used to manage network resources.

   T _____ F _____

7. NDS treats each resource as an object.

   T _____ F _____

LAB 9.5 UNDERSTANDING NDS CONTEXTS

Objectives

The goal of this lab is to increase your knowledge of NDS contexts. After completing this lab, you will be able to:

➤ Use the cx command to change contexts and view objects in the NDS tree

➤ Use typeless and typeful names

Materials Required

In this lab, you will need the following:

➤ Completion of Lab 9.4

➤ A computer named NW5_5 running Novell NetWare 5.0 Server

➤ A computer running Windows 95/98 and the Novell Client 32 software

➤ A functioning network connection between the two computers

ACTIVITY

1. Go to the Windows 95/98 client computer and log on to the Novell NetWare 5.0 Server computer as Admin.

2. Click **Start**, point to **Programs**, and then click **MS-DOS Prompt**. The MS-DOS Prompt window opens.

3. At the MS-DOS prompt, type **cx** and then press **Enter**.

4. Record the output. _____

   _____

5. To change the current context to SALES, type **cx SALES** and press **Enter**. The current context appears on the next line.

6. To change the context to [Root], type **cx ..** (or **cx /r**), and then press **Enter**.

7. Record the output. _____

   _____

8. To change contexts using a typeless name, type **cx .SALES.NW5_O** and then press **Enter**. The new context appears on the next line.

9. Change to the [Root] container.

10. Record the command you entered in order to change to the [Root] container. _____
_____

11. To change contexts using a typeful name, type **cx .OU=SALES.O=NW5_O** and then press **Enter**. The new context appears on the next line.

12. In order to move up one level to the parent container, type **cx .** and press **Enter**.

13. Record the output. _____
_____

14. To view a tree listing of the current context, type **cx /a/t** and then press **Enter.**

15. Record the output.

16. To view a tree listing of [Root] and all containers, type **cx /a/r/t** and then press **Enter.**

17. Record the result.

18. From the client computer, log off the server computer.

Review Questions

1. Define the term context. _____
_____
_____
_____

2. Which of the following commands will change to the [Root] container?

   a. cx /r

   b. cx \r

   c. cx root

   d. cx [Root]

3. Which of the following commands will change to a container called PROD?

    a. cd PROD

    b. md PROD

    c. cx /r/PROD

    d. cx PROD

4. Which of the following are examples of NDS typeless names? Choose two.

    a. OU=PROD.OU=USA.O=FIRM_A

    b. PROD.USA.FIRM_A

    c. O=FIRM_B

5. Which of the following are examples of NDS typeful names? Choose two.

    a. PROD.USA.FIRM_A

    b. OU=PROD.OU=USA.O=FIRM_A

    c. O=FIRM_B

    d. FIRM_B

6. It is possible to create a container object in a leaf object.

    T _____ F _____

7. It is possible to create a leaf object in a container object.

    T _____ F _____

Note   Most of the time you will use NDS typeless names. However, for some NDS activities, you must enter the typeful names. For example, in order to save changes to a volume, you must enter the typeful name of the Admin user.

CHAPTER TEN

NETWORKING WITH UNIX

Labs included in this chapter

➤ Lab 10.1 User and Group Management

➤ Lab 10.2 Managing Directories and Files

➤ Lab 10.3 Understanding UNIX Help

➤ Lab 10.4 Understanding Wildcard Symbols, Redirection Symbols and the Pipe Symbol

➤ Lab 10.5 Navigating the UNIX File System

LAB 10.1 USER AND GROUP MANAGEMENT

Objectives

The goal of this lab is to help you learn how to manage users and groups within UNIX. After completing this lab, you will be able to:

➤ Add, modify, and delete user accounts

➤ Add, modify, and delete group accounts

➤ Log in using new usernames

Materials Required

This lab will require the following:

➤ A computer, with a host name of UNIX1, running Linux Red Hat 6.1

➤ Knowledge of the root user's password

ACTIVITY

1. Boot the computer.

2. At the UNIX1 login prompt, type **root** and press **Enter**. The Password prompt appears on the next line.

3. At the Password prompt, type the correct password for the **root** user and press **Enter**. A prompt similar to [root@UNIX1 /root]# appears.

4. At the prompt, type **cd /** and press **Enter**. The prompt changes to [root@UNIX1 /]#. The / in the prompt indicates that this is the root, or top-level, directory.

5. In order to create a user, type **useradd Zac** and press **Enter**. The prompt returns indicating that the command was successfully executed.

6. In order to create a group, type **groupadd Managers** and press **Enter**. The prompt returns.

7. In order to create another group, type **groupadd Employees** and press **Enter**. The prompt returns.

8. In order to designate the Managers group as Zac's primary group and the Employees group as Zac's supplementary group, type **usermod -g Managers -G Employees Zac** and press **Enter**. The prompt returns. The Zac user account has been added to both groups.

9. In order to verify that Zac has been added to both groups, type **groups Zac** and press **Enter**. A list of groups to which Zac belongs is displayed on the screen.

10. In order to change the default shell for `Zac` to the Bourne shell (`/bin/sh`), type **usermod —s /bin/sh Zac** and press **Enter**.

11. In order to change the password for `Zac`, type **passwd Zac** and press **Enter**. On the next line you see the message `Changing password for user Zac` followed by the prompt `New UNIX password`.

12. At the `New UNIX password` prompt, type a password and press **Enter**. The message `New UNIX password` appears.

13. At the `New UNIX password` prompt, type the password a second time (to confirm it) and press **Enter**.

14. To log out as the `root` user type **logout** and press **Enter**. The `UNIX1 login` prompt appears.

15. At the `UNIX1 login` prompt, type `Zac` and press **Enter**.

16. At the `Password` prompt, type the correct password for `Zac` and press **Enter**. (Use the password you typed in Steps 12 and 13.) The prompt appears.

17. What directory name appears in the prompt? _____

_____

18. To display information about the user `Zac`, type **finger Zac** and press **Enter**.

19. Read the output of the **finger** command, and record when `Zac` logged on last. _____

_____

20. Log out as the user `Zac`.

21. Log back in as `root`.

22. In order to prevent Zac from logging in, type **usermod —L Zac** and press **Enter**. The **—L** option locks the account. (You could use the **—U** option to unlock the account.)

23. In order to delete the user `Zac`, type **userdel Zac** and press **Enter**.

24. In order to delete the group `Managers`, type **groupdel Managers** and press **Enter**.

25. Using **useradd**, create a new user account for yourself. For the user name, use your first initial followed by your last name. For example, if your name is "Todd Meadors," then your username would be `TMeadors`. Record your username here: _____

_____

26. Log out as the `root` user.

10

Review Questions

1. Bob has a Linux user account. He is going on vacation for two weeks. As a UNIX system administrator, you need to make sure no one uses his account during his absence. What is the best way to keep his user information intact, while at the same time preventing others from logging in with Bob's username?

    a. Delete Bob's primary group.

    b. Use the `usermod` command to unlock his account.

    c. Use the `usermod` command to lock his account.

    d. Change his default shell.

    e. Use the `finger` command to delete his account.

2. Users should always write down their passwords.

    T _____ F_____

3. A user can be a member of multiple groups.

    T _____ F _____

4. What is the command used to add a user in Linux?

    a. `useradd`

    b. `groupadd`

    c. `usermod`

    d. `groupmod`

    e. `createuser`

5. Which of the following commands gives information about the user?

    a. `groupdel`

    b. `mkdir`

    c. `ls`

    d. `finger`

    e. `ps`

6. What is the purpose of typing a user's password twice when changing passwords? _____

    _____

    _____

    _____

7. The `groupadd` command allows you to add a user.

    T _____ F _____

LAB 10.2 MANAGING DIRECTORIES AND FILES

Objectives

The goal of this lab is to help you understand how to manage UNIX directories and files. After completing this lab, you will be able to:

➤ Create and remove a directory

➤ Create, view, and remove a file

Materials Required

This lab will require the following:

➤ A computer with a host name of UNIX1, running Linux Red Hat 6.1 or another version of UNIX

➤ Knowledge of the **root** user's password

➤ Completion of Lab 10.1

ACTIVITY

10

1. Boot the computer.

2. Log in using your own username (which you created in Step 25 of Lab 10.1).

3. At the prompt, type **pwd** and press **Enter**. What is the output of the **pwd** command? _____

4. In order to create a directory called payroll, type **mkdir payroll**. The prompt returns, indicating that the command was successfully executed.

5. In order to view files and folders in the current directory, type **ls** and press **Enter**. What is the output of the **ls** command?

    _____

6. In order to create a file called **file2.txt**, type **echo "Hello" > file2.txt** and press **Enter**. The prompt returns. (Note that the > symbol is known as a redirection symbol and is explained in Lab 10.4.)

7. In order to view the contents of the file, type **cat file2.txt** and press **Enter**. The prompt returns.

8. In order to append the text **The end!** to file2.txt, type **echo "The end >> file2.txt** and press **Enter**. (The >> symbol is another redirection symbol and is explained in Lab 10.4.)

9. Repeat Step 7 and record the output.

    _____

10. In order to copy `file2.txt` to a file called `file3.txt`, type `cp file2.txt file3.txt` and press **Enter**.

11. Type `ls —l` and press **Enter**. A long list of files and directories appears.

12. Write a brief description of the output generated by the `ls —l` command.

    _____

    _____

    _____

13. In order to create another directory, type `mkdir prod` and press **Enter**. The prompt returns, indicating that the command was successfully executed.

14. In order to delete the directory called `prod`, type `rmdir prod` and press **Enter**. The prompt returns, indicating that the command was successfully executed.

15. In order to change the payroll directory, created in Step 4, type `cd payroll` and press **Enter**. What does the prompt look like now?

    _____

16. Enter `pwd` and press **Enter**. What is the output?

    _____

17. In order to create a hidden file, type `echo "Hidden file" > .file-is-hidden` and press **Enter**. The prompt returns, indicating that the command was successfully executed.

18. Type `ls` and press **Enter**. Do you see the file `.file-is-hidden` in the list? _____

19. Type `ls —a` and press **Enter**. Do you see the file `.file-is-hidden` in the list? _____

20. Type `cd..` and press **Enter**. This moves your current directory up one level.

21. In order to rename `file2.txt` as `file7.txt`, type `mv file2.txt file7.txt` and press **Enter**. The prompt returns, indicating that the command was successfully executed.

22. Type `ls` and press **Enter**. Do you see `file2.txt` or `file7.txt` in the output? _____

23. In order to remove `file7.txt`, type `rm file7.txt` and press **Enter**. The prompt returns, indicating that the command was successfully executed.

24. Type `ls` and press **Enter**. Do you see `file7.txt` in the output?

    _____

25. Log out.

Review Questions

1. You can create a directory within a file in Linux.

   T _____ F _____

2. You can create a file within a directory.

   T _____ F _____

3. What command would you type in order to change to the SALES directory?

   a. mv SALES

   b. pwd

   c. cd SALES

   d. ls SALES

   e. rmdir SALES

4. Which of the following commands is used to create a directory?

   a. mkdir

   b. md

   c. cd

   d. chdir

   e. rmdir

5. The rmdir command is used to remove a file.

   T _____ F _____

6. The rm command is used to remove a directory.

   T _____ F _____

7. To view hidden files, use the —a option on the ls command.

   T _____ F _____

 The names of hidden files in UNIX begin with a period.

LAB 10.3 UNDERSTANDING UNIX HELP

Objectives

The goal of this lab is to help you learn about UNIX Help by executing the man command. After completing this lab, you will be able to:

➤ Find Help on any UNIX command

➤ Execute the man command

Materials Required

This lab will require the following:

➤ A computer with a host name of UNIX1, running Linux Red Hat 6.1 or another version of UNIX

ACTIVITY

1. Boot the computer and log in as the user you created in Step 25 of Lab 10.1.

2. In order to display information about the **cd** command, type **man cd** and press **Enter**. Information (known as a "man page") for the **cd** command appears. Read the **man** page and then record the purpose of the **cd** command.

   _____

3. Press **Q** to quit the **man** page and return to the prompt.

4. Type **man ls** and press **Enter**. The Help pages for the **ls** command appear. What is the purpose of the –a option?

   _____

5. Press **Q** to quit the **man** page and return to the prompt.

6. Type **man rm** and press **Enter**. The Help pages for the **rm** command appear.

7. Use the **Spacebar** to scroll down one page at a time until you locate the option for removing the contents of directories recursively. Record that option here. _____

8. In order to search for text within a **man** page, type **man ls** and press **Enter**. The **man** pages for the **ls** command appear on the screen.

9. Now you can search for information about inodes within the **ls** Help page. To create the correct command, you type a forward slash (/) followed by the text you want to search for. So to search for inode, type **/inode** and press **Enter**. The screen scrolls to the word inode in the **man** page for the **ls** command.

10. Press **Q** to quit and return to the prompt.

11. Log out as the **root** user.

Review Questions

1. Use the **man** command to find a definition for the **who** command. Record the definition here. Also, identify and discuss one option for the **who** command._____

   _____

   _____

   _____

2. Use the **man** command to find a definition for the **date** command. Record the definition here. Also, identify and discuss one option for the **date** command. _____

_____

_____

3. Use the **man** command to find a definition for the **grep** command. Record the definition here. Also, identify and discuss one option for the **grep** command. _____

_____

_____

4. Use the **man** command to find a definition for the **cat** command. Record the definition here. Also, identify and discuss one option for the **cat** command.

_____

_____

_____

5. Use the **man** command to find a definition for the **uname** command. Record the definition here. Also, identify and discuss one option for the **uname** command. _____

_____

_____

10

6. Use the **man** command to record a definition for the **kill** command. Record the definition here. Also, identify and discuss one option for the **kill** command. _____

_____

_____

7. Use the **man** command to find a definition for the **tail** command. Record the definition here. Also, identify and discuss one option for the **tail** command. _____

_____

_____

8. Use the **man** command to find a definition for the **wc** command. Record the definition here. Also, identify and discuss one option for the **wc** command.

_____

_____

_____

9. Use the **man** command to find a definition for the **ps** command. Record the definition here. Also, identify and discuss one option for the **ps** command.

_____

_____

_____

10. Use the **man** command to find a definition for the **echo** command. Record the definition here. Also, identify and discuss one option for the **echo** command. _____

_____

_____

LAB 10.4 UNDERSTANDING WILDCARD SYMBOLS, REDIRECTION SYMBOLS AND THE PIPE SYMBOL

Objectives

The intent of this lab is to help you understand how to use UNIX wildcard symbols. After completing this lab, you will be able to:

➤ Use the wildcard symbol * for multiple characters

➤ Use the wildcard symbol ? for a single character

➤ Use the redirection symbol > to create a new file

➤ Use the redirection symbol >> to append text to an existing file

➤ Use the pipe symbol | to connect two commands

Materials Required

In this lab, you will need the following:

➤ A computer with a host name of **UNIX1** running Linux Red Hat 6.1 or another version of **UNIX**

➤ Completion of Lab 10.2

ACTIVITY

1. Log on as the **root** user.

2. To change directory locations to the payroll directory, type **cd \payroll** and press **Enter**. The prompt changes to reflect the current directory (\payroll).

3. In order to demonstrate how wildcards work in this lab, you need to create about 10 files. To do this, you will create one file and then copy it to create the other nine files. In order to create the first file, type **echo "Hi" > Jan01.txt** and press **Enter**. The prompt returns. The redirection symbol > is used to redirect output to a newly created file.

4. In order to copy the contents of the file to a new file, type **cp Jan01.txt Jun05.txt** and press **Enter**. The prompt returns, indicating that the command was successfully executed.

5. Use the **cp** command to create files with the following names: `Jul01.txt, Jan14.dat, Jul14.dat, Feb14.txt, Jan06.txt, Feb07.txt, Apr28.txt,` and `Oct27.dat`. For example, to create the file called `Feb07.txt`, type **cp Jan01.txt Feb07.txt** and press **Enter**.

6. Wildcarding is the process of using two special symbols, * and ?, to display a subset of the file and directories in a given directory. In order to wildcard multiple characters, use the * symbol. In order to wildcard a single character position, use the **?** symbol. In order to see the files that begin with the letter A, type **ls A*** and press **Enter**.

7. Record the result. _____

   _____

8. In order see the files for February, type **ls Feb*** and press **Enter**.

9. Record the result. _____

   _____

10. In order to see the files for the 14th of the month, type **ls ???14*** and press **Enter**.

11. Record the result. _____

    _____

12. In order to see the files for January that end in txt, type **ls Jan*.txt** and press **Enter**.

13. Record the result. _____

    _____

14. In order to see the files with a 7 in the fifth position, type **ls ?????7*** and press **Enter**.

15. Record the result. _____

    _____

16. In order to use the pipe symbol to count the total number of users logged on, type **who | wc -l** and press **Enter**. (Note that the **wc** command with the **-l** option actually counts the number of lines generated by the **who** command.)

17. Record the result. _____

    _____

18. Now you will use the pipe symbol to find your user name in the list of users currently logged in. For example, if your user name is zac, then you would type **who | grep zac** and press Enter. Type the correct command for your user name and press **Enter**.

19. Record the result. _____

    _____

10

20. In order to gain a greater understanding of the pipe symbol, you will need to create a file with multiple lines of text. In the next few steps, you will create a file of five lines, with each line containing a single number. Initially, the numbers will be arranged in random order. In a later step, you will sort the numbers in the file using the | symbol. To create the file, type **echo "5" > unsort.dat** and press **Enter**.

21. The redirection symbol **>>** is used to append data to an existing file. Text already in the file will be left intact. To append text to the file **unsort.dat**, type **echo "3" >> unsort.dat** and press **Enter**.

22. To append text to the file **unsort.dat**, type **echo "1" >> unsort.dat** and press **Enter**.

23. To append text to the file **unsort.dat**, type **echo "4" >> unsort.dat** and press **Enter**.

24. To append text to the file **unsort.dat**, type **echo "2" >> unsort.dat** and press **Enter**.

25. In order to view the contents of the **unsort.dat** file, type **cat unsort.dat** and press **Enter**.

26. Record the result. _____
    _____
    _____

27. Now that you have created the file, you can sort it. In order to sort the file, type **cat unsort.dat | sort** and press **Enter**. The pipe symbol redirects the output from the command on the left-hand side of the pipe symbol to the command on the right-hand side of the pipe symbol. (Note that you could also sort the file without using the pipe symbol, as follows: **sort unsort.dat**.)

28. In order to sort the file and place the sorted output into a new file, type **sort unsort.dat > sort.dat** and press **Enter**.

29. To see the contents of the new file, type **cat sort.dat** and press **Enter**.

30. Record the result. _____
    _____
    _____

31. What is the difference between the result you recorded in Step 26 and the result you recorded in Step 30. _____
    _____

32. Next, you will use the pipe symbol for one of its most common uses, displaying a lot of output one screen at a time. In order to demonstrate this feature, you first need to create a file containing 41 lines of text. Repeat Steps 21 through 24 of this lab nine more times to create a file that contains 41 lines of text.

33. In order to view the contents of the **unsort.dat** file, type **cat unsort.dat** and press **Enter**.

34. Count the lines of text displayed on the screen.

35. Do you see all the contents of the file? _____

_____

36. In order to view the contents one page at a time, type **cat unsort.dat | more** and press **Enter**. One screenful of contents is displayed.

37. Press the **Spacebar** to display the remainder of the file.

38. Do you see all the contents of the file now? _____

_____

39. Log out.

Review Questions

1. What is the purpose of wildcard characters?

_____

_____

_____

2. In order to wildcard a single character position, use the * symbol.
   T _____ F _____

3. Which of the following is known as the pipe symbol?
   a. ?
   b. >
   c. >>
   d. *
   e. |

4. In order to wildcard multiple character positions, use the ? symbol.
   T _____ F _____

5. The symbol used to create a new file is <.
   T _____ F _____

6. Explain the purpose of the pipe symbol.

_____

_____

_____

10

LAB 10.5 NAVIGATING THE UNIX FILE SYSTEM

Objectives

The intent of this lab is to teach you how to navigate the UNIX file system. After completing this lab, you will be able to:

➤ Create directories

➤ Change directories

➤ Explain how to change directory locations using the full pathname and the partial pathname

Materials Required

In this lab, you will need the following:

➤ A computer with a host name of **UNIX1** running Linux Red Hat 6.1 or another version of UNIX

➤ Completion of Lab 10.1

ACTIVITY

1. Log on as the user you created in Lab 10.1.

2. In order to create a directory named **sales**, type **mkdir sales** and press **Enter**. The prompt returns.

3. In order to change to the **sales** directory, type **cd sales** and press **Enter**. The prompt changes to reflect the current directory (**sales**). To verify your current directory, type **pwd** and press **Enter**. What output do you see? _____

   _____

4. Create a directory named **monthly**. Write the full command you used.

   _____

5. Create another directory named **yearly**. Write the full command you used. _____

   _____

6. To view a list of files and directories, type **ls** and press **Enter**. You should see two directories. What are the directory names?

   _____

7. In order to change to the monthly directory, type **cd monthly** and press **Enter**. The prompt changes to reflect the current directory (monthly), and output appears on the screen. Record the output.

   _____

   _____

8. To verify your current directory, type **pwd** and press **Enter**. What output do you see? _____

9. Draw the file system hierarchy from your home directory. Draw lines extending down from one directory level to the next directory level. Write the name of each directory. _____

_____

_____

_____

10. To change to the **root** directory, type **cd /** and press **Enter**. The prompt changes to reflect the root, or top, of the file system.

11. To change to your home directory, you need to type **/home** followed by your username. For example, if your username is **tmeadors**, then you would type **cd /home/tmeadors** and then press **Enter**. Use the appropriate command now to change to your home directory. The prompt changes to reflect your new directory location. Write the full command you used to change to your home directory. _____

_____

12. Change to the **sales** directory, which you created in Step 2. The prompt changes to reflect the current directory (**sales**). Write the full command you used. _____

_____

13. Change to the **yearly** directory, which you created in Step 5. The prompt changes to reflect the new directory location. Write the full command you used. _____

_____

14. To change to the **monthly** directory from within the **yearly** directory, type **cd ../monthly** and press **Enter**. The directories **monthly** and **yearly** are peer, or sibling, directories. Peer, or sibling, directories are directories that exist on the same level in the hierarchy; they have the same parent directory. The prompt changes to reflect the new directory location.

15. To verify your current directory, type **pwd** and press **Enter**. What output do you see? _____

_____

16. To change back to the **yearly** directory from within the **monthly** directory, type **cd ../yearly** and press **Enter**. The prompt changes to reflect the new directory location.

17. To verify your current directory, type **pwd** and press **Enter**. What output do you see? _____

_____

18. To change to the parent directory, type **cd ..** and press **Enter**. The prompt changes to reflect the new directory location. (The two dots represent the parent directory.)

19. To verify your current directory, type **pwd** and press **Enter**. What output do you see? _____

_____

20. Log out of the computer.

Review Questions

1. Define the term file system. _____

_____

_____

_____

2. In order to change directory locations, you can use the **mkdir** command.
   T _____ F _____

3. Peer, or sibling, directories are on equal hierarchical levels.
   T _____ F _____

4. The parent directory is represented by a single dot.
   T _____ F _____

5. The root symbol is represented by the / symbol.
   T _____ F _____

6. What is the top of the UNIX file system called?

   a. home

   b. parent

   c. root

   d. subdirectory

   e. child

Note

A UNIX full path begins at the root directory. For example, /home/zac is a full path. Notice the / before home. A UNIX partial path does not begin at the root directory. For example, /home/zac is a partial path. Notice the absence of / before home.

CHAPTER ELEVEN

NETWORKING WITH TCP/IP AND THE INTERNET

Labs included in this chapter

➤ Lab 11.1 Understanding TCP/IP Addresses, Network Classes and Subnet Masks

➤ Lab 11.2 Understanding the Purpose of the Default Gateway

➤ Lab 11.3 Understanding the TCP/IP Hosts File

➤ Lab 11.4 Configuring Dynamic Host Configuration Protocol (DHCP)

➤ Lab 11.5 Configuring Domain Name Service (DNS)

➤ Lab 11.6 Configuring Windows Internet Naming Service (WINS)

➤ Lab 11.7 Using FTP

➤ Lab 11.8 Understanding Port Numbers

LAB 11.1 UNDERSTANDING TCP/IP ADDRESSES, NETWORK CLASSES AND SUBNET MASKS

Objectives

The goal of this lab is to help you understand TCP/IP addresses, network classes, and subnetting. After completing this lab, you will be able to:

➤ Use the Windows calculator program to convert decimal numbers into binary numbers

➤ Use the Windows calculator program to determine if two TCP/IP addresses are on the same subnet

➤ Determine the default subnet address for an IP address

➤ Determine the network class for an IP address

Materials Required

This lab will require the following:

➤ A computer with Windows 95, Windows 98, or Windows NT installed

➤ Pencil and paper

ACTIVITY

1. Boot the Windows computer.

2. Click **Start** and then click **Run**. The Run dialog box opens.

3. In the Open text box, type **calc**, and press **Enter**. The Calculator application opens.

4. Click **View** on the menu bar, and then click **Scientific**. Additional functions appear on the calculator. Using this calculator, you can enter a decimal number and then click binary to see the number's binary equivalent. In order to convert an IP address into binary, you must convert one octet at a time. In this case, you want to convert the IP address 165.100.90.5 into binary form.

5. Verify that the **Dec** option button is selected. This ensures that when you first type a number, it will be displayed in decimal (regular base 10) form.

6. Type **165** and click **Bin**. The first number in the octet, 165, is converted into binary. Record the binary number. _____

7. Now you are ready to convert the second octet, 100, into binary. Click **Dec**, type **100**, and click **Bin**. Record the binary number.

_____

8. Convert the third octet to binary. Record the binary number.

_____

9. Convert the fourth octet to binary. Record the binary number.

_____

10. Convert the IP address 165.100.90.5 into binary form. Record the result.

_____

11. Record the network class for the IP address 165.100.90.5.

_____

12. Record the default subnet mask for the IP address 165.100.90.5.

_____

13. Convert the IP address 214.55.11.2 into binary form. Record the result.

_____

14. Record the network class for the IP address 214.55.11.2.

_____

15. Record the default subnet mask for the IP address 214.55.11.2.

_____

16. Convert the IP address 15.19.50.135 into binary form. Record the result.

_____

17. Record the network class for the IP address 15.19.50.135.

_____

18. Record the default subnet mask for the IP 15.19.50.135.

_____

11

Review Questions

1. Which of the following IP addresses belongs to a Class B network?
   a. 150.110.10.133
   b. 4.5.112.32
   c. 41.8.78.117
   d. 241.45.12.19

2. The IP address 255.255.255.255 is a valid IP address.

   T _____ F _____

3. A Class C network can have up to 65,534 hosts per network.

   T _____ F _____

4. A Class A IP address has a number between 192 and 223 as its first octet.

   T _____ F _____

5. The total possible number of class A networks is 2,000,000.

   T _____ F _____

6. What network class is reserved for multicasting?

   a. A

   b. B

   c. C

   d. D

   e. E

7. The IP address 277.11.18.29 is a valid IP address.

   T _____ F _____

LAB 11.2 UNDERSTANDING THE PURPOSE OF THE DEFAULT GATEWAY

Objectives

The goal of this lab is to help you understand the purpose of the default gateway. After completing this lab, you will be able to:

➤ Identify the purpose of the default gateway

➤ Identify which default gateway to use on a network

Materials Required

This lab will require the following:

➤ Completion of Lab 11.1

➤ Pencil and paper

ACTIVITY

1. Review the following scenario: Computers A, B, and C (shown in Figure 11-1) are on two networks with the default subnet mask used for all three computers. The NIC(s) inserted in each computer have the IP addresses indicated in the figure. Computer B has two IP addresses because it has two NICs.

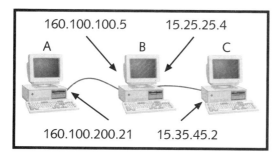

Figure 11-1 Computers A, B, and C on a network

2. Record the correct default gateway for computer A.

_____

3. Record the correct default gateway for computer C.

_____

4. Record the network portion of the IP address for computer A.

_____

5. Record the network portion of the IP address for computer C.

_____

6. Record whether the computer is acting as the default gateway or router.

_____

7. Review the following scenario: computers A and C (shown in Figure 11-2) are on two networks, with the default subnet mask used for all three computers. Assume that item "B" is a dedicated Cisco router.

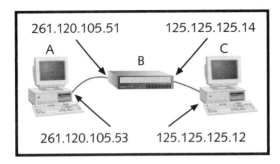

261.120.105.51   125.125.125.14

A   C
        B

261.120.105.53   125.125.125.12

Figure 11-2 Computers A and C on two networks

8. Record the correct default gateway for computer A.

_____

9. Record the correct default gateway for computer C.

_____

10. Record the network portion of the IP address for computer A.

_____

11. Record the network portion of the IP address for computer C.

_____

Review Questions

1. What is the purpose of the default gateway? _____

_____

_____

_____

2. The default gateway is also known as a router.
   T _____ F _____

3. Define the term dotted decimal notation. _____

_____

_____

_____

4. An IP address is 32 bits in size.
   T _____ F _____

5. The IP address 127 is used exclusively for loopback testing.
   T _____ F _____

6. The network portion of the IP address is common to all nodes on one network.
   T _____ F _____

7. The host portion of the IP address is unique to each node on one network.
   T _____ F _____

LAB 11.3 UNDERSTANDING THE TCP/IP HOSTS FILE

Objectives

The intent of this lab is to help you understand the purpose of the TCP/IP hosts file. After completing this lab, you will be able to:

➤ Identify the purpose of the hosts file

➤ Modify the hosts file

➤ Connect to another computer using its host name

Materials Required

In this lab, you will need the following:

➤ A computer running Windows NT Server 4.0 with an IP address of 160.100.100.112

➤ A computer running Linux Redhat 6.1 with an IP address of 160.100.100.200

➤ A functioning network connection between the two computers

11

ACTIVITY

1. Log on to the Windows NT Server 4.0 computer as an administrator.

2. Click **Start**, point to **Programs**, and click **Command Prompt**. The Command Prompt dialog box opens.

3. In order to change the current directory location, type **cd\winnt\ system32\drivers\etc**, and press **Enter**. The prompt changes to reflect the new directory location. On a Windows NT Server 4.0 or Workstation 4.0 computer, this directory contains the hosts file. On a UNIX system, the hosts file is located in the /etc directory; the full name is /etc/hosts.

4. In order to modify the hosts file, type **edit hosts**, and press **Enter**. The hosts file opens with text on the screen.

5. Scroll to the bottom of the screen and type **160.100.100.200 unixbox**, and press **Enter**. Make sure the entry is on a line by itself and that there is no pound sign (#) in front of the entry. (A pound sign at the beginning of

a line indicates a comment.) Also, make sure there is at least one space before the word unixbox. Refer to Figure 11-3 for a sample screen shot of the hosts file after the entry has been added.

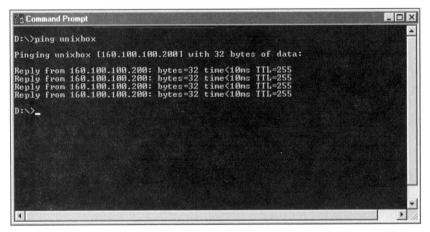

Figure 11-3 A sample screen shot of a hosts file with a host entry

6. Now, you can try using the host name in a command. Type **ping unixbox**, and press **Enter**. Four successful replies appear on the screen. Figure 11-4 shows a successful attempt to ping a computer with an IP address of 160.100.100.200 by using its hostname.

```
D:\>ping unixbox

Pinging unixbox [160.100.100.200] with 32 bytes of data:

Reply from 160.100.100.200: bytes=32 time<10ms TTL=255
Reply from 160.100.100.200: bytes=32 time<10ms TTL=255
Reply from 160.100.100.200: bytes=32 time<10ms TTL=255
Reply from 160.100.100.200: bytes=32 time<10ms TTL=255

D:\>_
```

Figure 11-4 Pinging a computer using the host name specified in the hosts file

7. Now that you have tested the connection using the host name, edit the hosts file and insert the symbol used for a comment at the beginning of the entry you entered in Step 5. What symbol did you use to comment the entry? (Note that "comment" is often used as a verb in this way, to indicate changing part of a file into a comment.) _____

_____

8. Close the Command Prompt dialog box.

9. Log off the Windows NT Server computer.

> Your instructor may tell you to use different IP addresses than those specified in this project.
>
> **Note**

Review Questions

1. What is the purpose of the hosts file? _____

_____

_____

_____

2. Which of the following symbols indicates a comment in the hosts file?

    a. ?

    b. >

    c. <<

    d. *

    e. #

3. What is the purpose of the alias in the hosts file? _____

_____

_____

_____

11

4. Given the following hosts file, what is the IP address of the computer named NT1?

```
# This hosts file was created by Todd Meadors on
11/26/1999.
160.12.122.13   NT2   NT2alias
156.11.21.145   UNIX5 goober
123.14.11.214   NT1   PDC1
44.112.133.15   NTWS5   FIVE
```

   a. 160.12.122.13

   b. 156.11.21.145

   c. 123.14.11.214

   d. 44.112.133.15

5. Given the following hosts file, what is the alias of the computer with the IP address of 156.11.21.145?

```
# This hosts file was created by Todd Meadors on
11/26/1999.
160.12.122.13   NT2   NT2alias
156.11.21.145   UNIX5 cactus
123.14.11.214   NT1   PDC1
44.112.133.15   NTWS5   FIVE
```

   a. FIVE

   b. NTWS5

   c. cactus

   d. NT2alias

   e. UNIX5

6. Zac is working on a UNIX computer system. He needs to ping 10 computers each day to make sure they are up and running. He cannot remember the IP address of all 10 computers. What file should he alter to resolve the host names to the IP addresses?

   a. `\etc\hosts.txt`

   b. `/etc/lmhosts`

   c. `/etc/hosts`

   d. `/hosts`

   e. `/etc/hostnames.txt`

7. Each node on the same network must have a unique IP address.

T _____ F _____

LAB 11.4 CONFIGURING DYNAMIC HOST CONFIGURATION PROTOCOL (DHCP)

Objectives

The intent of this lab is to teach you about DHCP. After completing this lab, you will be able to:

➤ Configure DHCP to automatically distribute the IP addresses and subnet masks to other computers

➤ Renew the IP address on a DHCP client

Materials Required

In this lab, you will need the following:

➤ A computer running Windows NT Server 4.0 with DHCP installed

➤ A computer running Windows NT Workstation 4.0 without a specific IP address

➤ A functioning network connection between the two computers

11

ACTIVITY

1. Log on to the Windows NT Server as an administrator.

2. Click **Start**, point to **Programs**, point to **Administrative Tools (Common)**, and click **DHCP Manager**. The DHCP Manager dialog box opens.

3. Click **Local Machine**, click **Scope**, click **Create**. The Scope Properties - (Local) dialog box opens.

4. Now you can begin configuring this DHCP server to automatically give out IP addresses from 160.100.100.5 to 160.100.100.55; the server should also distribute the default subnet mask of 255.255.0.0. Click the **Start Address** text box, type **160.100.100.5**, and press **Enter**.

5. In the End Address text box, type **160.100.100.55**, and press **Enter**.

6. In the Subnet Mask text box, type **255.255.0.0**, and press **Enter**. (See Figure 11-5.)

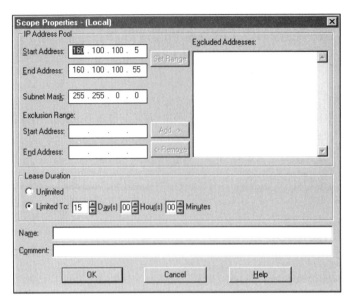

Figure 11-5 Scope Properties - (Local) dialog box

7. Click **OK**. The DHCP Manager dialog box returns.

8. Next, you will test the DHCP server. To begin testing, log on to the Windows NT workstation as an administrator. A workstation can receive an IP address by "renewing" the IP address.

9. Click **Start**, point to **Programs**, click **Command Prompt**. The Command Prompt dialog box opens.

10. In order to obtain an IP address, type **ipconfig /renew**, and press **Enter**. Record the IP address that is listed on the screen.

_____

11. Log off both computers.

Review Questions

1. What is the purpose of DHCP? _____

_____

_____

_____

2. DHCP can automatically distribute an IP address.

   T _____ F _____

3. DHCP can automatically distribute a subnet mask.

   T _____ F _____

4. With DHCP, the network administrator does not have to manually keep track of IP addresses for every node.

   T _____ F _____

5. What is the purpose of the DHCP lease? _____

   _____

   _____

   _____

6. DHCP was developed by the IETF to replace BOOTP.

   T _____ F _____

7. A client computer can either have its IP address manually entered or be set to automatically obtain an IP address from a DHCP server.

   T _____ F _____

A Windows NT server running DHCP Manager is called the DHCP server. A Windows NT workstation cannot be a DHCP server.

11

LAB 11.5 CONFIGURING DOMAIN NAME SERVICE (DNS)

Objectives

The intent of this lab is to teach you about DNS. After completing this lab, you will be able to:

➤ Add a DNS server to DNS

➤ Add a DNS zone

➤ Add a DNS host

➤ Configure a computer to refer to the DNS server

➤ Access a computer using its DNS name

Materials Required

In this lab, you will need the following:

➤ A computer running Windows NT Server 4.0 with DNS installed and an IP address of 160.100.100.112

➤ A computer running Windows NT Workstation 4.0 with an IP address of 160.100.100.186

➤ A functioning network connection between the two computers

ACTIVITY

1. Log on to the Windows NT Server as an administrator.

2. Click **Start**, point to **Programs**, point to **Administrative Tools (Common)**, and click **DNS Manager**. The Domain Name Service Manager dialog box opens. Note the Server List icon, which indicates the current list of DNS servers if there are any. If there are no entries beneath the Server List icon, then there are no DNS servers.

3. In the left pane, right-click **Server List**, and then click **New Server**. The Add DNS Server dialog box opens. You will use this dialog box to add a DNS server that will maintain a database that matches host names to their corresponding IP addresses.

4. In the DNS Server box, type **160.100.100.112**, and click **OK**. An entry for the server appears beneath the Server List icon, indicating that a DNS server has been added. You also see a Cache entry beneath the DNS server entry. The Cache entry contains the IP addresses of the main DNS servers on the Internet. These are called root servers because they are the top-level servers in the DNS database. Each DNS server manages a collection of computers known as a zone. In the next step you will create a new zone.

5. Right-click the server entry **160.100.100.112**, and click **Create New Zone**. The Create New Zone for 160.100.100.112 dialog box opens with two options: Primary and Secondary. Each zone must have a primary server; this is the server that workstations use in order to resolve host names to IP addresses.

6. Click **Primary** and then click **Next**. The Zone Information dialog box opens.

7. In the Zone name text box, type **little.com**, press **Enter**, and then click the zone name text box. The entry little.com.dns appears in the Zone file text box.

8. Click **Next** and then click **Finish**. You return to the Domain Name Service Manager dialog box. In the left pane, below the Server List icon, you will see an icon for the little.com zone.

9. Verify that little.com is selected in the left pane, and then examine the information in the right pane. This pane contains entries that are called records. There are many types of records in DNS. Each record contains a name, a description of the type of record it is, and the data within the record. Each type of record has a specific function. Two record types appear by default. They are the SOA and the NS record types. SOA stands for Start of Authority. NS stands for the Name Server record type, and it identifies the DNS server.

10. Next, you need to specify a host name and IP address for the selected record. Right-click **little.com**, and click **New Host**. The New Host dialog box opens. In the Host name text box, type **cactus**. (The name "cactus" is arbitrary.)

11. In the IP address text box, type **160.100.100.186**, and then click **Add Host**. A new host record type, A, appears in the Zone Info section of the Domain Name Service Manager dialog box, as shown in Figure 11-6. The A indicates that it is an Address record type. A record type of A is required for each host name entry. This completes the process of adding the Windows NT Workstation to the domain named little.com. The Windows NT Workstation can be accessed by its Fully Qualified Domain Name (FQDN), which is cactus.little.com and is easier to remember than the numerical address 160.100.100.186.

11

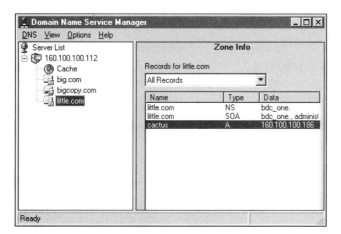

Figure 11-6 Completed Domain Name Service Manager dialog box

12. Next, you need to configure your workstation to refer to the DNS server. Log on to the Windows NT workstation.

13. Right-click **Network Neighborhood** and then click **Properties**. The Network dialog box opens.

14. Click **Protocols**, click **TCP/IP Protocol**, and then click **Properties**. The Microsoft TCP/IP Properties dialog box opens.

15. Click **DNS**. The DNS properties dialog box opens.

16. In the DNS Service Search Order section, click **Add**. The TCP/IP DNS Server dialog box opens.

17. In the DNS Server text box, type **160.100.100.112**, and then click **Add**. The TCP/IP DNS Server dialog box closes, but the DNS properties dialog box remains open. The IP address of the DNS Server appears in the DNS Service Search Order section. Now, the Windows NT workstation is configured to refer to the DNS server for domain names.

18. Click **OK** to close the Microsoft TCP/IP Properties dialog box. You return to the Network dialog box.

19. Click **OK** to close the Network dialog box.

20. In order to access the Windows NT workstation, using the DNS entry on the DNS server, go to the Command Prompt on the Windows NT Workstation computer.

21. Type **ping cactus.little.com**, and press **Enter**. The ping command should return four successful replies indicating the numerical IP address of cactus.little.com (160.100.100.186).

22. Log off both computers.

Review Questions

1. What is the purpose of a secondary name server? _____
   _____
   _____
   _____

2. A computer must have a Primary Name Server entry in order for it to use DNS.
   T _____ F _____

3. The root servers of the Internet are maintained by the InterNIC.
   T _____ F _____

4. Which of the following are examples of top-level domains? Choose all that apply.

   a. .com

   b. .gov

   c. .ibm

   d. .net

5. An address resource record type is identified with an A.

   T _____ F _____

6. The IN resource record refers to the Internet record class.

   T _____ F _____

7. What is the difference between the hosts file and DNS? _____

   _____

   _____

   _____

LAB 11.6 CONFIGURING WINDOWS INTERNET NAMING SERVICE (WINS)

11

Objectives

The intent of this lab is to teach you about WINS. After completing this lab, you will be able to:

➤ Install WINS

➤ Inspect the WINS database

➤ Configure a client computer to use WINS for NetBIOS names

➤ Configure DNS to use WINS

Materials Required

In this lab, you will need the following:

➤ A computer running Windows NT Server 4.0 with DNS installed and an IP address of 160.100.100.112

➤ The Windows NT Server 4.0 installation CD

➤ A computer running Windows NT Workstation 4.0 with an IP address of 160.100.100.186 and a NetBIOS name of WS-A

➤ A functioning network connection between the two computers

➤ Completion of Lab 11-5

ACTIVITY

1. Log on to the Windows NT Server as an administrator. The Windows desktop appears.

2. Right-click on **Network Neighborhood** and click **Properties**. The Network dialog box appears.

3. Click **Services**. The list of installed services appears in the Services list.

4. Click **Add**. The Select Network Service dialog box appears.

5. In the Network Services list, click **Windows Internet Name Service**.

6. Click **OK**. The Windows NT Setup dialog box appears with the drive letter of the CD-ROM and the path to the I386 folder.

7. Make sure the drive letter is correct.

8. Insert the Windows NT Server 4.0 installation CD into the CD-ROM drive.

9. Click **Continue**. The Windows NT Setup program copies files to the hard disk drive. When complete, the Network dialog box reappears.

10. Click **Close**. The Network Settings Change dialog box appears.

11. Click **Yes** to restart the computer.

12. After the computer reboots, click **Start**, point to **Programs**, point to **Administrative tools (Common)** and verify that WINS Manager is now listed on this menu. This server is now considered a WINS server. WINS resolves NetBIOS, or computer, names to IP addresses. While WINS is similar to DNS, WINS maintains a dynamic database and DNS maintains a static database. Computer names will automatically be placed in the WINS database as the computers boot. With DNS, you need to add host names manually to the DNS server, as you saw in the previous lab when you added the Address record for the host name "cactus."

13. In order for a client computer to use WINS for NetBIOS name resolution, you now need to enable WINS resolution and add a Primary WINS server on the Windows NT workstation. Log on to the Windows NT Workstation computer.

14. Right click **Network Neighborhood**, and then click **Properties**. The Network dialog box opens.

15. Click **Protocols**, click **TCP/IP Protocol**, and then click **Properties**. The Microsoft TCP/IP Properties dialog box opens.

16. Click **WINS Address**. The WINS Properties dialog box opens.

17. In the Primary WINS Server text box, type **160.100.100.112**, and press **Enter**.

18. Select the **Enable DNS for Windows Resolution** check box. This allows the workstation to use the WINS server for FQDN name resolution. At this point, the workstation is configured to use the WINS server for name resolution. In order for the server computer to accept NetBIOS instead of host names, you must configure DNS to perform a WINS lookup; a lookup occurs when the server finds the IP address in its database. Go to the Windows NT Server computer and access **DNS Manager.** The Domain Name Service Manager dialog box opens.

19. Double-click **Server List**, double-click on the server's IP address (160.100.100.112), right-click the **little.com** domain, and then click **Properties**.

20. The Zone Properties dialog box for the selected domain opens with four tabs.

21. Click the **WINS Lookup** tab. The WINS Lookup properties dialog box opens.

22. Select the **Use WINS Resolution** check box. This indicates that you want to allow DNS, which is a static database, to use WINS, which is a dynamic database.

23. Click **Add**. The Add WINS Server dialog box opens.

24. Type **160.100.100.112**, and press **Enter**.

25. Click **OK**. The Domain Name Service Manager dialog box reappears. At this point, the DNS server has been configured to perform a WINS lookup.

26. On the Windows NT Server computer, open the Command Prompt window.

27. Type **ping ws-a.little.com**, and press **Enter**. This ping command should return four successful replies, indicating that you have just accessed the computer via its NetBIOS name instead of its host name or its IP address. The DNS server did not have an entry for "ws-a," but it was able to search the dynamic WINS database to find the IP address; this resulted in a successful reply to the ping command.

28. Log off both computers.

Review Questions

1. What is the purpose of WINS? _____
_____
_____
_____

2. WINS is a static database.
   T _____ F _____

3. DNS is a dynamic database.
   T _____ F _____

4. WINS is used to resolve host names to IP addresses.
   T _____ F _____

5. DNS is used to resolve NetBIOS names to IP addresses.
   T _____ F _____

6. WINS guarantees unique NetBIOS names for each node on the network.
   T _____ F _____

LAB 11.7 USING FTP

Objective

The intent of this lab is to teach you about FTP. After completing this lab, you will be able to:

➤ Use FTP

Materials Required

In this lab, you will need the following:

➤ A computer running Windows NT Server 4.0, named NT_BOSS_BOX, with Internet Information Server 2.0, 3.0 or 4.0 installed

➤ A computer running Windows NT Workstation 4.0

➤ A functioning network connection between the two computers

ACTIVITY

1. Create three text files (containing any text) and save them in the \inetpub\ftproot folder of the Windows NT Server computer.

2. Log on to the Windows NT Workstation computer as an administrator.

3. Click **Start**, point to **Programs**, and then click **Command Prompt**. The Command Prompt dialog box opens.

4. Type **ftp nt_boss_box**, and press **Enter**. You will see messages indicating that you are connected to the server. On the third line, you see the following prompt: User (nt_boss_box.dekalb.tec.ga.us:(none)):. Here you can enter a username. In the next step, you will connect to the FTP server, using the username "anonymous."

5. At the User (nt_boss_box.dekalb.tec.ga.us:(none)): prompt, type **anonymous**, and press **Enter**. A password prompt appears. When logged in as anonymous, you can use any password; however it is customary to use your last name or e-mail address as the password.

6. Type your last name, and press **Enter**.

7. A message indicating you are logged on as the anonymous user appears. Then the ftp> prompt appears.

8. Type **ls**, and press **Enter**. The list of files you saved to the \inetpub\ftproot directory appears.

9. Record the files that are displayed. _____
   _____

10. Attempt to copy one of the files to the workstation's hard disk by entering an FTP get command. For example, to copy the file named monkey.txt, type **get monkey.txt** at the ftp> prompt, and then press **Enter**. You should see a message indicating that the command was successful. Note that you need read access on the FTP server to retrieve a file from it; this is the default setting, so there is no need to change anything.

11

11. Record the name of the file you retrieved. _____

12. You can use the put command to upload files to the FTP site. Type **help put**, and press **Enter**.

13. To disconnect from the FTP session, type **bye** at the ftp> prompt, and press **Enter**. The C: prompt appears.

14. Log off the Windows NT Workstation computer.

Review Questions

1. What is the purpose of FTP? _____
   _____
   _____
   _____

2. With FTP, you can retrieve files from an FTP site.

   T _____ F _____

3. FTP stands for File Transfer Protocol.

   T _____ F _____

4. With FTP, you can upload files to an FTP site.

   T _____ F _____

5. What type of access do you need to get a file from an FTP site?

   a. read

   b. write

   c. delete

   d. execute

IIS 2.0 can be installed as a service via the Network dialog box. Once you do this, the computer is then called an FTP Server. The steps for installing it are similar to those for installing WINS (which are described in Lab 11.6).

LAB 11.8 UNDERSTANDING PORT NUMBERS

Objectives

The intent of this lab is to teach you about port numbers. After completing this lab, you will be able to:

➤ Identify default port numbers for several services

➤ Modify a service's default port numbers

➤ Connect to a service using a nondefault port number

Materials Required

In this lab, you will need the following:

➤ A computer running Windows NT Server 4.0, named BDC_ONE, with Internet Information Server 2.0 installed

➤ Internet Explorer installed on the Windows NT Server 4.0 computer

ACTIVITY

1. Log on to the Windows NT Server computer.

2. Click **Start**, point to **Programs**, click **Microsoft Internet Server (Common)**, and then click **Internet Service Manager**.

3. The Microsoft Internet Service Manager dialog box opens with WWW, FTP, and Gopher services displayed. In the following steps you will change the port numbers for the WWW, or World Wide Web, service. (This service allows you to connect to Web servers by using Internet Explorer or another Web browser.)

4. Double-click the entry for the WWW service. The WWW Service Properties dialog box for your server opens, as shown in Figure 11-7.

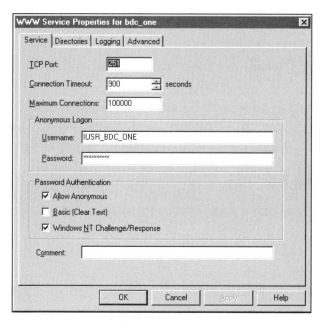

Figure 11-7 WWW Service Properties dialog box

5. Record the value in the TCP port text box. _____

6. In the TCP Port box, type **251**, press **Enter**, and then click **OK**. A message box appears, indicating that you must restart the WWW service in order for the change to take effect.

7. Click **OK**. The Microsoft Internet Service Manager dialog box reappears. You can stop and restart the WWW service here.

8. Right-click the WWW service entry, and click **Stop**. The state of the service changes to Stopped.

9. In order to start the service, right-click the WWW service entry and click **Start**. The state of the service changes to Running. The default port value has now been changed to 251. Any computer using Internet Explorer to access this server must use this new port number.

10. In order to verify the change, start Internet Explorer on the same computer.

11. In the Address box, enter **http://bdc_one**, and press **Enter**. The name following the two forward slashes, "bdc_one" is the name of the Windows NT Server computer. After a moment, an error occurs. Record the error message you see. _____

12. Click **OK**. The error message box closes.

13. In order to access the default Web site on this server, using a port other than the default one, you need to type the server's name followed by a colon and the correct port number. In this case, you need to type **http://bdc_one:251** in the Address box, and press **Enter**. The server's default Web page opens.

14. Explain why the Web site opened in Step 13, but not in Step 11.

   _____

15. Close **Internet Explorer** and close **Microsoft Internet Service Manager**.

16. Log off the Windows NT 4.0 Server computer.

Review Questions

1. What symbol is used to separate the computer name from the port number in a URL?

   a. ;

   b. :

   c. .

   d. #

2. The default port number for Telnet is 21.
   T _____ F _____

3. What is a socket? _____

   _____

   _____

4. The default port number for FTP is 23.
   T _____ F _____

5. The default port number for HTTP is 80.
   T _____ F _____

6. The default port number for SNMP is 161.
   T _____ F _____

CHAPTER TWELVE

TROUBLESHOOTING NETWORK PROBLEMS

Labs included in this chapter

➤ Lab 12.1 Using the Ping Command to Troubleshoot a TCP/IP Network
➤ Lab 12.2 Troubleshooting a Malfunctioning NIC
➤ Lab 12.3 Troubleshooting a Malfunctioning 10BaseT Cable
➤ Lab 12.4 Troubleshooting a Malfunctioning Hub

LAB 12.1 USING THE PING COMMAND TO TROUBLESHOOT A TCP/IP NETWORK

Objectives

The goal of this lab is to help you use the Ping command to locate any problems in a TCP/IP network. After completing this lab, you will be able to:

➤ Use the Ping command to determine the source of problems in a TCP/IP network

➤ Isolate a problem by following a logical methodology

Materials Required

This lab will require the following:

➤ A Windows NT 4.0 Server computer with two NICs, configured as a router, with a computer name of SERVER1; the IP address of the first NIC should be 160.100.100.100; the IP address of the second NIC should be 170.100.100.100

➤ Two 10BaseT hubs, each connected to a different NIC on the router

➤ A Windows NT 4.0 Workstation computer named WSI that is connected to one of the hubs with a 10BaseT cable; the computer's IP address should be 160.100.100.6

➤ A Windows NT 4.0 Workstation named WS2 connected to one of the hubs with a 10BaseT cable; the computer's IP address should be 170.100.100.7

ACTIVITY

1. Review the layout and IP addresses of the network in Figure 12-1.

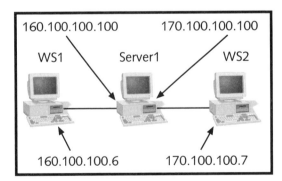

Figure 12-1 Network layout

2. Now you can determine if WS2 (which has an IP address of 170.100.100.7) is up and running. Review the following problem-isolation methodology. (Do not perform the steps yet; simply review them so that you understand how you will go about troubleshooting the network.)

   a. Log on to the computer named WS1. Ping the local computer's local loopback address to ensure that its NIC is working properly. (The term "local computer" refers to the computer you are logged on to—in this case, WS1.)

   b. Ping the local computer's IP address to ensure that TCP/IP is working properly.

   c. Ping the near side of the router to ensure that the connection between 160.100.100.6 and 160.100.100.100 is operating properly. The term "near side" refers to the segment of the router that is on the same network as the local computer.

   d. Ping the far side of the router to ensure that the connection through the router is operating properly; specifically, this test ensures that the connection between 160.100.100.6 and 170.100.100.100 is functional. The term "far side" refers to the segment of the router that is not on the same network as the local computer.

   e. Ping a computer on the network segment on the far side of the router; in this situation, the computer on the far side of the router is the computer named WS2. This ensures connectivity all the way from 160.100.100.6 (which is WS1) to 170.100.100.7 (which is WS2).

The following steps walk you through the commands procedure outlined above. For each ping test, the Ping command will issue a message indicating either success or failure. If the Ping command returns an error at any step, you can assume that the previous connections work. The problem then lies with the connection at the particular step that produced the error.

3. Boot all three computers.

4. Log on to WS1, which has the IP address of 160.100.100.6, as an administrator.

5. Click **Start**, point to **Programs**, and click **Command Prompt**. The Command Prompt dialog box opens.

6. Now, you can implement the methodology outlined in Step 2. In order to determine if the local computer's NIC is operating correctly, type **ping 127.0.0.1** and press **Enter**. Record the output of the Ping command and indicate whether or not it was successful. _____

12

7. In order to determine if TCP/IP is operating properly, type **ping 160.100.100.6** and press **Enter**. Record the output of the Ping command and indicate whether or not it was successful. _____

8. In order to determine if the connection to the near side of the router is operating properly, type **ping 160.100.100.100** and press **Enter**. Record the output of the Ping command and indicate whether or not it was successful. _____

9. In order to determine if the router is operating properly, type **ping 170.100.100.100** and press **Enter**. Record the output of the Ping command and indicate whether or not it was successful. _____

10. In order to determine if a computer on the network segment on the far side of the router is operating properly, type **ping 170.100.100.7** and press **Enter**. Record the output of the Ping command and indicate whether or not it was successful. _____

11. Unplug the cable that is connected to the NIC with the IP address of 170.100.100.100.

12. Repeat Steps 6 through 10. Which step failed? _____
Record the error message resulting from the failure?

13. Plug in the cable you unplugged in Step 11.

Review Questions

1. If you cannot access the near side of the router, then you cannot access the far side of the router.
T _____ F _____

2. Outline the steps for determining connectivity for a computer on a network segment other than your own. _____

3. In regard to the troubleshooting steps, if the Ping command fails on any of the steps, the problem lies with the previous step.
T _____ F _____

4. If you cannot ping the local computer's loopback address, then you won't be able to ping any computer on the network.
T _____ F _____

LAB 12.2 TROUBLESHOOTING A MALFUNCTIONING NIC

Objective

The intent of this lab is to teach you how to troubleshoot a malfunctioning NIC. After completing this lab, you will be able to:

➤ Isolate a malfunctioning NIC

Materials Required

In this lab, you will need the following:

➤ Pencil and paper

ACTIVITY

1. Review the following scenario:

   You are working the help desk at your company and receive a call from a user who cannot access the network. The user says that she was able to connect to the network yesterday, and there have been no changes to her computer software or hardware since then. Her coworkers in adjacent cubicles can access the network. The user has a Windows 95 computer, and the computer is operating properly. You need to methodically troubleshoot the problem by following the steps outlined below. For each step, answer the accompanying question.

2. You tell the user to right-click on My Computer and click Properties. The System Properties dialog box opens. Next, you tell the user to click the Device Manager tab. A list of devices on the computer opens. Next, you tell the user to double-click on Network Adapters. The name of the network adapter appears. The user tells you that she sees a red circle with a diagonal line through it next to the network adapter icon. What does this tell you? _____

   _____

3. You tell the user to look for any other red circles with diagonal lines through them, next to the other devices listed. The user sees no other red circle next to any other device listed. Does this increase the likelihood that the network adapter is the problem? _____

   _____

4. Suppose the user sees a red circle with a diagonal line through it next to the icon for the LPT1 printer port. Could this explain why the user could not access the network? _____ Explain your answer.

   _____

   _____

12

5. You tell the user to check the status lights on the network adapter. You also tell her to look at the back of the computer for a connector that looks similar to a modular phone plug; this is the RJ-45 connector. What information do you hope to acquire from this step?

_____

_____

6. The user informs you that the lights are not on. What does this tell you?

_____

_____

7. Explain how you can test the cable to ensure that it is working properly?

_____

8. Tell the user she should replace the cable plugged into the back of her computer with a cable from a coworker's computer that can access the network. How will this help isolate the problem? _____

_____

9. The user switches cables and says that she cannot access the network even after switching cables. What component is definitely the problem?

_____

10. Tell the user to replace her coworker's cable. Why should the user replace the coworker's cable? _____

_____

11. You send a technician to the site. What replacement part should the technician bring with her? _____

_____

Review Questions

1. Explain why you should investigate a problem thoroughly before you simply replace a component. _____

_____

_____

_____

2. After you replace a component, you should test it to ensure that the new component works.
   T _____ F _____

3. Suppose that in Step 8 the coworker's cable had not worked. Which of the following two problems might be possible explanations for why the user's network connection wasn't working?

   a. The user's cable is malfunctioning.
   b. The network adapter is malfunctioning.
   c. The coworker's cable is malfunctioning.
   d. The hub could be down.

4. A NIC can cause trouble on a network if it is using the same IRQ as another device.

T _____ F _____

5. In Window 95, what does a red circle with a line through it indicate?

_____

_____

_____

LAB 12.3 TROUBLESHOOTING A MALFUNCTIONING 10BASET CABLE

Objective

The intent of this lab is to help you understand how to troubleshoot a malfunctioning cable. After completing this lab, you will be able to:

➤ Isolate a malfunctioning cable

Materials Required

In this lab, you will need the following:

➤ Completion of Lab 12.2

➤ Pencil and paper

ACTIVITY

1. Review the following scenario:

   You are working the help desk at your company and, as in Project 12-2, receive a call from a user who cannot access the network. His coworkers sitting in adjacent cubicles can access the network. The user has a Windows NT workstation computer, and it is working properly. You need to methodically troubleshoot the problem by following these steps. Remember to consider these questions as a checklist of items you could ask a user.

2. First, you ask if anything has been changed. If the user says nothing has been changed, then proceed with the steps below; otherwise, investigate the change. Why would you ask the user if he changed anything? _____

   _____

3. Explain how you would proceed if the user admitted to changing something? _____

   _____

4. You need to determine if the network adapter, or NIC, is working properly. Tell the user to look in Event Viewer. To do this, tell the user to click **Start**, point to Programs, and then click Administrative Tools (Common). The Event Viewer dialog box opens. Event Viewer has three logs: the System, the Security, and the Application log. The System log

appears by default with a list of entries. In Event Viewer, there are three types of messages: stop errors, warning messages, and informational messages. You tell the user to look for any entries that have icons that look like red stop signs. These are called stop errors and will cause activity associated with them to stop. This does not necessarily mean that the computer won't work. The user sees no stop errors. Do you think the network adapter is the problem? _____

_____

5. You tell the user to check the status lights on the network adapter. You tell him to look at the back of the computer for a connector that looks similar to a modular phone plug; this is the RJ-45 connector. The user says the lights are not on. Is the cable possibly the problem? _____

_____

6. You ask the user to unplug the RJ-45 connector and plug it back in. What is the purpose of this step? _____

_____

7. You ask the user if the lights are on. The user informs you the lights are still off. What does this tell you? _____

8. You ask the user to switch cables with a coworker. After the user switches the cable, the user informs you that the lights are now on. What does this tell you? _____

_____

9. You ask the user to attempt to access the network. The user informs you that he can access the network now. You ask the user to replace the coworker's cable and explain that you will send a technician with a replacement part. What replacement part should the technician bring with her?

_____

_____

Review Questions

1. If a cable is incorrectly wired, it will not allow access to the network.
   T _____ F _____
2. A cable can be tested with a cable tester to ensure that it's properly made.
   T _____ F _____
3. What types of messages would you see in Windows NT Event Viewer?

_____

_____

_____

4. Discuss the importance of following a logical methodology when troubleshooting a problem. _____

_____

_____

_____

LAB 12.4 TROUBLESHOOTING A MALFUNCTIONING HUB

Objective

The intent of this lab is to teach you how to troubleshoot a malfunctioning hub. After completing this lab, you will be able to:

➤ Isolate a malfunctioning hub

Materials Required

In this lab, you will need the following:

➤ Paper and pencil

ACTIVITY

1. Review the following scenario:

   You are working as a network manager for a small company. The company is divided into three departments, with the computers in each department arranged in a star topology. Each department has two hubs, with six workstations connected to each hub. All the hubs are connected, allowing all three departments to communicate with each other over the network. You are paged by a user who has suddenly lost access to the network. Concurrently, you hear your name being called over the loudspeaker to contact another user within the same department as the first user. Then you get a call from a third user in the same department who is unable to access the network. You need to methodically troubleshoot the problem by following these steps. Again, think of this as a checklist.

2. You contact the users, and log them on to your database of user problems. Do you think it is important to keep a tracking log of user problems on the computer? _____ Explain your answer.

   _____

   _____

3. You ask if anything has been changed. The users inform you that they did not change anything. You visit the department and notice that all computers on one of the two hubs appear to be working. The users with computers on the second hub are the ones who contacted you earlier. What could be the problem? _____ Explain your answer.

   _____

   _____

4. You inspect the lights on the hub and see that none of the lights on any of the ports of the hub are on. What does this tell you?

   _____

   _____

   _____

12

5. You inspect the power cord and notice it is plugged in correctly. Would the hub necessarily be the problem if the power cord was unplugged from the wall outlet? _____

_____

6. Connect one of the computers from the first hub to the suspect hub. This computer cannot gain network access now. What does this tell you?

_____

_____

7. You replace the hub and verify that the computers connected to the new hub can access the network at this point. Summarize the steps you took to isolate the problem. _____

_____

_____

_____

Review Questions

1. Identify the symptoms in this lab scenario that indicated a malfunctioning hub. _____

_____

_____

_____

2. Why is it important to test your changes when troubleshooting?

_____

_____

_____

3. Why is it important to ask a user if there have been any changes to his or her computer recently? _____

_____

_____

_____

4. Computers connected to a malfunctioning hub will be unable to access the network.
   T _____ F _____

5. If the users described in the preceding scenario were from different departments, would you consider other possible sources for the problem? Explain why or why not. _____

_____

_____

_____

CHAPTER THIRTEEN

MAINTAINING AND UPGRADING A NETWORK

Labs included in this chapter

➤ Lab 13.1 Using Windows NT Performance Monitor

➤ Lab 13.2 Client Upgrades

➤ Lab 13.3 Upgrading a 10Base-T LAN to a 100Base-T LAN

➤ Lab 13.4 Researching Network Solutions

LAB 13.1 USING WINDOWS NT PERFORMANCE MONITOR

Objectives

The goal of this lab is to help you use Windows NT Performance Monitor to track network and computer usage. After completing this lab, you will be able to:

➤ Use Windows NT Performance Monitor

➤ Create and save files in Performance Monitor

➤ Monitor network and computer activity

Materials Required

This lab will require the following:

➤ A Windows NT 4.0 Server computer

➤ A Windows NT 4.0 Workstation computer

➤ A functioning network connection between the two computers

ACTIVITY

1. Log on to the Windows NT Server as an administrator.

2. Click **Start**, point to **Programs**, click **Administrative Tools (Common)**, and then click **Performance Monitor**. The Performance Monitor dialog box opens. You can use Performance Monitor to monitor the use of certain network resources and to establish baseline readings for your network. You can then compare these baseline statistics to statistics taken in the future, to determine if network performance is degrading. In order to create a chart to track network performance, you must add objects and counters to Performance Monitor. An object is a computer or network resource such as the processor, the network adapter, or the disk. Counters are variables related to an object. For example, the object named Processor has a counter, named %Processor Time, which measures the processor's activity. To add an object, click **Edit** and click **Add to Chart**. The Add to Chart dialog box opens. In this dialog box, you see the computer name, a list of objects, and a list of counters.

3. The Processor object is the default object, and %Processor Time is the default counter for the Processor object. In order to display a brief explanation of the counter called %Processor Time, click **Explain**. A Counter Definition dialog box is appended to the Add to Chart dialog box.

4. Review the definition and, in your own words, record a definition for the %Processor Time counter. _____

_____

_____

5. Now, you will actually add the counter to the chart in order to display statistical performance in the form of a graph. To do so, click **Add** and click **Done**. The Performance Monitor dialog box now displays a graphical chart of the Processor object and its %Processor Time counter.

6. In order to add statistical information about the NIC resource, you will need to add the Network Interface object. To do so, click **Edit** and click **Add to Chart**. The Add to Chart dialog box opens. In the Object list, scroll up and then click the entry for **Network Interface**. The default counter, Bytes Total/sec, appears.

7. To display information about this counter, click **Explain**. A Counter Definition dialog box is appended to the Add to Chart dialog box.

8. Review the definition of Bytes Total/sec and, in your own words, record a definition for Bytes Total/sec below. _____

_____

_____

9. Click **Add** and then click **Done**. The Performance Monitor dialog box now adds the Network Interface counter to the chart.

10. Close Performance Monitor and log off.

Review Questions

13

1. Define the term baseline. _____

_____

_____

_____

2. Define the term asset management. _____

_____

_____

_____

3. Define the term change management. _____

_____

_____

_____

4. Baselining can assist you in predicting the impact of major changes to your network.

   T _____ F _____

5. As part of asset management, which of the following items regarding a network computer should you record? Choose all that apply.

    a. software version

    b. location of computer in the network

    c. configuration files

    d. serial number and model number

    e. technical support contact for software

6. As part of asset management, you should keep records about changes and upgrades to printers.
    T _____ F _____

7. It is important to keep the change management system current.
    T _____ F _____

8. You should keep track of hardware and software additions but not removals.
    T _____ F _____

LAB 13.2 CLIENT UPGRADES

Objective
The intent of this lab is to teach you how to upgrade a client computer. After completing this lab, you will be able to:

➤ Upgrade a Novell Client

Materials Required
In this lab, you will need the following:

➤ A Windows 95/98 computer with the Novell 4.11 Client software loaded

➤ A Novell NetWare 5.0 Server computer

➤ The Novell Client Software installation CD

ACTIVITY

1. In this lab, you upgrade a Novell NetWare 4.11 client computer to a Novell NetWare 5.0 client. Boot the Windows 95/98 client. The Windows desktop opens.

2. Insert the Novell Client Software installation CD into the CD-ROM drive of the Windows 95/98 client computer. Double-click the icon representing the CD-ROM drive. The WinSetup – Novell Clients dialog box opens. A list of languages appears; the one you select will be used for the installation.

3. Click **English**. The WinSetup – Novell Clients dialog box refreshes and displays a list of clients you can install.

4. Click **Windows 95/98 Client**. A list of Windows 95/98 components available for installation appears in the WinSetup – Novell Clients dialog box.

5. Click **Install Novell Client**. The Novell Client for Windows 95/98 License Agreement dialog box opens.

6. Review the agreement and click **Yes**. The Welcome to the Novell Client for Windows 95/98 Install dialog box opens. There are two installation options: Typical, which is selected by default, and Custom, for more advanced users.

7. To perform a Typical installation, click **Install**. The Novell Client for Windows 95/98 Installation dialog box opens, informing you of the status of the installation process. Once the installation process is complete, the Novell Client for Windows 95/98 Installation program indicates that you must reboot in order for the client installation process to complete.

8. Click **Reboot**. The computer restarts.

9. Once the computer has restarted, you can then log in to the Novell Server 5.0 computer using the new client software.

Review Questions

1. Define the term software upgrade. _____

_____

_____

2. Define the term patch. _____

13

_____

_____

3. Microsoft uses the term service pack to refer to patches for Windows NT.
   T _____ F _____

4. You should always apply a patch while users are logged on.
   T _____ F _____

5. Describe the difference between an application upgrade and a network operating system upgrade. _____

_____

_____

6. Which of the following refers to the process of reversing a software upgrade?
   a. service pack
   b. backing up
   c. backleveling
   d. upgrade

Lab 13.3 Upgrading a 10Base-T LAN to a 100Base-T LAN

Objective

The intent of this lab is to teach you how to perform an upgrade from a 10Base-T-hub–based LAN to a faster 100Base-T-switch-based LAN. You will need to perform a cable upgrade in this lab as well. After completing this lab, you will be able to:

➤ Upgrade a LAN from 10Base-T to 100Base-T

Materials Required

In this lab, you will need the following:

➤ Completion of all labs in Chapter 4 of this book

➤ A 100Base-T switch

➤ A two-node LAN with a Windows NT 4.0 Server computer and a Windows NT 4.0 Workstation computer

➤ Each computer connected to a 10Base-T hub with CAT 3 cable

➤ Crimpers and at least 25 feet of CAT 5 cable

➤ NICs in each computer capable of 100 Mbps transmission

➤ A watch with a second hand

Activity

1. Power on both computers. Log on to the workstation. Note the time. Access the server by clicking on its icon in Network Neighborhood. Record the time it takes to access the server. _____

2. Shutdown both computers and power them off.

3. Unplug the power to the 10Base-T hub.

4. Remove the CAT 3 cables from each NIC and each port on the 10Base-T hub.

5. Create two new cables using the CAT 5 cable. See Lab 4-5 of Chapter 4 for instructions on correctly creating a cable.

6. Use the cable tester to test the cables. Refer to Step 4 of Lab 4-2 for complete instructions.

7. Plug the power cord of the 100Base-T switch into a wall outlet.

8. Plug one end of one cable into the NIC of the server. Plug the other end into the 100Base-T switch. The port lights on the hub should turn on, as should the lights on the NIC.

9. Repeat Step 8 for the workstation.

10. Power on both computers.

11. Log on to the workstation. Note the time. Access the server by clicking on its icon in Network Neighborhood. Record the time it took to access the server. _____ You should notice an increase in network activity as compared to Step 1.

Review Questions

1. You should upgrade all cable segments at once.
   T _____ F _____

2. There are companies that specialize in installing network cable.
   T _____ F _____

3. The most comprehensive and complex network hardware upgrade is a backbone upgrade.
   T _____ F _____

4. Identify at least three key issues to consider when justifying a backbone upgrade. _____
   _____
   _____
   _____

5. Give at least three examples of backbone upgrades. _____
   _____
   _____
   _____

6. You should document the existing cable prior to an upgrade.
   T _____ F _____

13

LAB 13.4 RESEARCHING NETWORK SOLUTIONS

Objectives

The intent of this lab is to teach you how to research networking solutions. You will accomplish this goal by visiting the Web sites of several networking companies and reviewing business case studies about their solutions. After completing this lab, you will be able to:

➤ Review case studies of networking companies

➤ Identify the needs of the customer in a case study

➤ Identify the solutions provided by the networking companies

Materials Required

In this lab, you will need the following:

➤ Pencil and paper

➤ A Windows 95/98 computer with an Internet connection

ACTIVITY

1. Boot the Windows computer.

2. Open the Web browser.

3. To review case studies for Novell, go to **www.novell.com/showcase**, then click **Go**. You see a list of case studies that demonstrate how Novell products have helped Novell customers.

4. Review a case study of your choice. Record the name of the customer and type of business you reviewed. _____

5. In your own words, record background information on the company.

_____

_____

_____

6. In your own words, record the business need or challenge for the company.

_____

_____

_____

7. In your own words, record the Novell solution. Be sure to identify the software or hardware solution that was implemented.

_____

_____

_____

8. In your own words, record the results of the solution.

_____

_____

_____

9. To review case studies for Microsoft, go to **www.microsoft.com**.

10. Locate the Search text box on the Microsoft Web page. Look in the upper-left side of the Web page; the company's Web pages change frequently, so you may have to look around on the Web site. In the text box, type **case study** and press **Enter**. A list of case studies appears.

11. Review a case study of your choice. Record the name of the customer and their type of business you reviewed. _____

_____

12. In your own words, record background information on the company.

_____

_____

_____

13. In your own words, record the business need or challenge for the company.

_____

_____

_____

13

14. In your own words, record the Microsoft solution. Be sure to identify the software or hardware solution that was used.

_____

_____

_____

15. In your own words, record the results of the solution.

_____

_____

_____

16. Close your Web browser.

Review Questions

1. You work as a network manager, and you are thinking about upgrading to a different network operating system. Explain how use of the Internet could assist you in your research. _____

_____

_____

_____

2. How can newgroups aid you in researching a new network solution?

_____

_____

_____

3. Explain how networking trends could increase your concern for network security. _____

_____

_____

_____

4. Discuss some of the trends in networking technology today. _____

_____

_____

_____

5. When considering upgrading to a new network operating system (NOS) you should go ahead and install the new NOS on production systems without testing it or researching it.

T _____ F _____

ENSURING INTEGRITY AND AVAILABILITY

Labs included in this chapter

➤ Lab 14.1 Viruses

➤ Lab 14.2 Universal Power Supplies (UPSs)

➤ Lab 14.3 Implementing RAID Level 0 (Disk Striping)

➤ Lab 14.4 Implementing RAID Level 1 (Disk Mirroring)

➤ Lab 14.5 Implementing RAID Level 5 (Disk Striping with Parity)

➤ Lab 14.6 Understanding Backups

LAB **14.1** VIRUSES

Objective

The goal of this lab is to help you understand viruses. After completing this lab, you will be able to:

➤ Understand viruses

Materials Required

This lab will require the following:

➤ A Windows 98 computer with an Internet connection

➤ McAfee VirusScan software installed

ACTIVITY

1. Boot the Windows 98 computer. First, in order to gain an understanding of virus-related terms, you will access the Webopedia Web site.

2. Start your browser and go to **www.webopedia.com**.

3. Search for the term macro virus, and record a definition in your own words.

   _____

   _____

   _____

4. Search for the term virus, and record a definition of worm (a type of virus) in your own words. _____

   _____

   _____

   _____

5. Search for the term Trojan horse, and record a definition in your own words.

   _____

   _____

   _____

6. Now you will try checking for a virus, using McAfee VirusScan. Start the McAfee Virus Scan program.

7. Scan the C: drive. The screen displays the number of files scanned, the names of any infected files, and the virus name and status. If you had any infected files, record the file name, the virus name, and the status.

   _____

8. Use the menu commands to display a list of viruses and information about each virus. Depending on your version of McAfee VirusScan, you may be able to use the Virus List command on the Tools menu to display this list.

9. Display specific information about each virus.

10. Scroll through the list of viruses. Note the virus characteristics, such as Memory resident, Encrypted, Polymorphic, Repairable, or Macro virus.

11. Scroll until you find a Memory-resident virus. Record the virus's name.

_____

12. Scroll until you find an Encrypted virus. Record the virus's name.

_____

13. Scroll until you find Macro virus. Record the virus's name.

_____

14. Close McAfee VirusScan.

Review Questions

1. Define the term encryption. _____

_____

_____

2. Define the term polymorphism. _____

_____

_____

3. Discuss the difference between signature scanning and integrity checking.

_____

_____

_____

4. Packaged software purchased from a store can contain a virus.
   T _____ F _____

5. The most common type of virus is a boot sector virus.
   T _____ F _____

6. Explain how a time-dependent virus works.

_____

_____

_____

LAB 14.2 UNIVERSAL POWER SUPPLIES (UPSS)

Objectives

The intent of this lab is to help you become familiar with UPSs. After completing this lab, you will be able to:

➤ Perform a cost comparison of UPSs

➤ Discuss the characteristics of UPSs

Materials Required

In this lab, you will need the following:

➤ Pencil and paper

➤ Access to a retail store that sells UPSs

ACTIVITY

1. Go to a retail computer store that sells UPSs.

2. Choose three UPS models. Complete the table below by writing down the vendor name, model number, price, and period of time that the UPS will keep a device running.

Vendor Name	Model Number	Time	Price

Review Questions

1. Define the term line conditioning. _____
_____
_____

2. Describe the difference between a UPS and a generator.
_____
_____
_____

3. Define the term surge. _____
_____
_____

4. Which of the following terms refers to a fluctuation in voltage levels caused by other devices on the network?

   a. brownout

   b. line noise

   c. volt drop

   d. blackout

5. Which of the following terms refers to a momentary decrease in voltage?

   a. blackout

   b. line noise

   c. volt drop

   d. brownout

6. Describe the difference between a standby UPS and an online UPS.

   _____

   _____

   _____

7. Electrical power is measured in volt–amps.

   T _____ F _____

LAB 14.3 IMPLEMENTING RAID LEVEL 0 (DISK STRIPING)

Objectives

The intent of this lab is to help you understand how to implement RAID Level 0, or disk striping. After completing this lab, you will be able to:

➤ Create a stripe set

➤ Identify the characteristics of RAID Level 0

Materials Required

In this lab, you will need the following:

➤ A Windows NT Server 4.0 computer with three hard disks installed

➤ At least 100 MB of free space on each hard disk

ACTIVITY

1. Log on to the Windows NT Server as an administrator.

2. Click **Start**, point to **Programs**, point to **Administrative Tools (Common)**, and click **Disk Administrator**. The Disk Administrator

window opens. (If you are running Disk Administrator for the first time, the utility indicates that it needs to write a signature record. Click **Yes** to write the signature record.) Disk Administrator displays drive letters and the amount of space that a drive letter occupies. It also displays the amount of free space on each disk.

3. In order to implement RAID Level 0, you need to select free space on at least two partitions. RAID Level 0 requires at least two disks. Click a partition labeled **Free Space** on disk 1, press **Ctrl** and click a partition labeled **Free Space** on disk 2. The two partitions are highlighted. Now you are ready to begin creating the stripe set.

4. Click **Partition** on the menu bar, and then click **Create Stripe Set...**. The Create Stripe Set dialog box opens.

5. In the Create stripe set of total size text box, type **100** and click **OK**. You return to the Disk Administrator window again; this time it displays a new drive letter for the stripe set. Record the drive letter. _____

6. Notice that the drive letter is the same on both disks. What is the size of just one of the partitions? _____

_____

7. Close Disk Administrator.

Review Questions

1. RAID Level 0 is also known as disk mirroring.
   T _____ F _____

2. Disk striping is fault tolerant.
   T _____ F _____

3. With RAID Level 0, if one disk fails, then all the data within it is inaccessible.
   T _____ F _____

4. RAID Level 0 improves performance because it involves multiple disk controllers.
   T _____ F _____

5. What is the block size used in disk striping?
   a. 128 KB
   b. 64 MB
   c. 64 KB
   d. 32 MB

6. RAID Level 0 should be used on a mission-critical system.

   T _____ F _____

7. Explain how RAID Level 0 works. _____

   _____

   _____

LAB 14.4 IMPLEMENTING RAID LEVEL 1 (DISK MIRRORING)

Objectives

The intent of this lab is to help you understand how to implement RAID Level 1, or disk mirroring. After completing this lab, you will be able to:

➤ Create a disk mirror

➤ Break a disk mirror

➤ Identify characteristics of RAID Level 1

Materials Required

In this lab, you will need the following:

➤ A Windows NT Server 4.0 computer with at least two hard disks installed

➤ At least 100 MB of free space on each hard disk

ACTIVITY

1. Log on to the Windows NT Server as an administrator.

2. Click **Start**, point to **Programs**, point to **Administrative Tools (Common)**, and click **Disk Administrator**. The Disk Administrator window opens.

3. In order to create a mirror, you must first create a partition. Click an area labeled **Free Space** on disk 1, click **Partition** on the menu bar, and click **Create**. The Confirm dialog box opens with a message indicating the partition may not be used by DOS. You will create it anyway.

4. Click **Yes**. The Create Primary Partition dialog box opens, displaying the minimum and maximum partition sizes.

5. In the Create partition of size text box, enter **40** and click **OK**. Disk Administrator displays a new drive letter and the size of the partition.

6. Record the drive letter. _____

14

7. Click the partition representing the new drive letter, click **Partition**, click **Commit Changes Now...** to write the changes to the Registry. The Confirm dialog box opens.

8. Click **Yes**. The Disk Administrator window opens, indicating that the disks were updated successfully.

9. Click **OK**. The Disk Administrator window displays the drives again. The partition has been created and its information saved to the Registry.

10. Next, you need to format the disk partition as an NTFS partition. (All RAID Levels support only the NTFS partition; they cannot use FAT.) Click the icon representing the disk partition (the partition you listed in Step 6), click **Tools** on the menu bar, and click **Format**. The Format dialog box opens.

11. Click **Start**. A warning box appears, indicating that the format process will erase all data on the partition.

12. Click **OK**. A progress bar appears at the bottom of the Format dialog box. Finally, the dialog box indicates that the process is complete.

13. Click **OK** and click **Close**.

14. In order to mirror this partition, click the partition (the one you recorded in Step 6), press **Ctrl** and click a partition labeled **Free Space** on the second disk. The two partitions are highlighted.

15. Click **Fault Tolerance** and then click **Establish Mirror**, in order to create a mirror. You have just created a mirror with two disk partitions of 40 MB each, for a total of 80 MB disk space utilized. No messages or dialog boxes confirm the change. Your Disk Administrator window should look similar to Figure 14-1. (In the figure, drive letter I represents the mirror on two separate disks.) Note that you don't have to specify a size when creating a disk mirror because a mirror is always the same size as the disk being mirrored. Now that the disks are mirrored, only 40 MB available remains for actual data storage. You could create folders and files under the new drive letter. The data would be copied to both partitions in the mirror. If one disk failed, you would have a complete copy on the second disk.

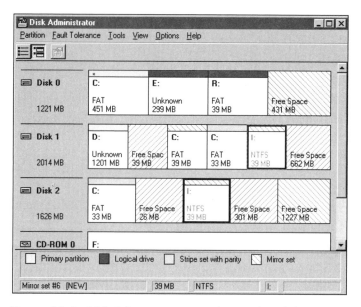

Figure 14-1   Disk Administrator window with a disk mirror

16. Now you can practice breaking, or disabling, a mirror—a process that would be necessary if one of the disks in the mirrored disk pair malfunctioned. Right-click on the mirror drive letter and click **Break Mirror**. The Confirm dialog box opens, indicating that two independent partitions will be created and that the second partition will now have a new drive letter. Both partitions will contain copies of any folders and files that were in the mirror.

17. Click **Yes**. The Disk Administrator window displays the additional disk partition. Record the new drive letter. _____

14

18. Close Disk Administrator.

Review Questions

1. Explain how disk mirroring works. _____
   _____
   _____

2. Disk mirroring requires three disks.
   T _____ F _____

3. RAID Level 1 is also known as disk mirroring.
   T _____ F _____

4. Jessie plans to implement disk mirroring. The disks are 100 MB each. After the disks are mirrored, how much disk space will be available for storing data.

    a. 100 MB

    b. 100 GB

    c. 100 KB

    d. none

5. Disk mirroring is fault tolerant.

    T _____ F _____

6. RAID Level 1 does not use any CPU resources.

    T _____ F _____

7. Define the term RAID. _____

_____

_____

Disk mirroring involves one disk controller managing two disks. Disk duplexing is a form of disk mirroring that employs one disk controller per disk. Disk duplexing is more fault tolerant than disk mirroring because if one disk controller fails with duplexing, you still can access the second disk with its own disk controller; in mirroring, if the single disk controller fails, then both disks are inaccessible.

LAB 14.5 IMPLEMENTING RAID LEVEL 5 (DISK STRIPING WITH PARITY)

Objectives

The intent of this lab is to help you understand how to implement RAID Level 5, or disk striping with parity. After completing this lab, you will be able to:

➤ Create a stripe set with parity

➤ Identify the characteristics of RAID Level 5

Materials Required

In this lab, you will need the following:

➤ A Windows NT Server 4.0 computer with at least three hard disks installed

➤ At least 100 MB of free space on each hard disk

ACTIVITY

Lab Activity

1. Log on to the Windows NT Server as an administrator.

2. Click **Start**, point to **Programs**, point to **Administrative Tools (Common)**, and click **Disk Administrator**. The Disk Administrator window opens.

3. RAID Level 5 requires at least three disks. In order to implement RAID Level 5, you need to use free space on at least three partitions. Click a partition labeled **Free Space** on disk 1; press **Ctrl** and click a partition labeled **Free Space** on disk 2. The two partitions are highlighted. Press **Ctrl** and click a partition labeled **Free Space** on disk 3. You should have three partitions on three separate disks highlighted.

4. Now you are ready to configure the system with RAID Level 5. Click **Fault Tolerance** on the menu bar, click **Create Stripe Set with Parity....** The Create Stripe Set with Parity dialog box opens.

5. In the **Create stripe set of total size** text box, type **100** and click **OK**. Disk Administrator displays a new drive letter for the Stripe Set with Parity. Record the drive letter. _____

6. Notice that the drive letter is the same on all three disks. What is the size of just one of the partitions? _____

7. Close Disk Administrator.

Review Questions

1. Explain the term fault tolerant. _____
   _____
   _____

2. RAID Level 5 requires three disks.
   T _____ F _____

3. Explain the difference between RAID Level 3 and RAID Level 5.
   _____
   _____
   _____

4. Define the term server mirroring. _____
   _____
   _____

5. Define the term parity. _____
   _____
   _____

14

6. Identify one advantage and one disadvantage of server clustering.

_____
_____
_____

7. Define the term hot swappable. _____

_____
_____

8. Suppose you have original data, expressed in bits, of 01110010. What is the parity bit when using odd parity?

a. 0

b. 1

LAB 14.6 UNDERSTANDING BACKUPS

Objectives

The intent of this lab is to help you learn how to back up data. In this lab, you will create a folder and two files on your hard drive, and then use the Microsoft backup utility to backup the files to a floppy drive. (Note that you would normally use a ZIP drive or some other backup device. Using the floppy drive here allows you to practice the necessary steps, regardless of whether you have a backup device installed.) You will also delete one of the files on the hard drive and then restore both files back to the hard drive from the floppy drive. After completing this lab, you will be able to:

➤ Back up data

➤ Restore data

➤ Identify the importance of data backups

Materials Required

In this lab, you will need the following:

➤ A Windows 98 computer with a floppy drive

➤ The ability to create a folder on the drive C

➤ The ability to create two text documents within the folder

➤ The ability to delete one of the text documents within the folder

ACTIVITY

1. Boot the Windows 98 computer.

2. Create a folder on drive C named **DATA**. Within this folder, create two files, named **test1.txt** and **test2.txt**.

3. In order to perform the backup, you need to start the Microsoft Backup program. Click **Start**, point to **Programs**, point to **Accessories**, point to **System Tools**, and click **Backup**. The Microsoft Backup dialog box opens. In the "What would you like to do?" option list, the selection **Create a new backup job** is selected by default.

4. Click **OK**. The Backup Wizard dialog box opens.

5. Click **Back up selected files, folders and drives**, and click **Next**. The Backup Wizard dialog box displays a list of drive letters. If you double-click on a folder in the left pane, the list of files within the folder will appear in the right pane; this works similarly to Microsoft Explorer.

6. In the left pane, entitled "What to back up," double-click the **C:** drive letter. The drive expands and displays a list of folders and files on it. Here you can select a folder (and the files it contains) by placing a check next to the folder's icon.

7. Click the check box to the left of the folder named DATA. The check box appears next to the folder in both the left and right panes. The DATA folder, and all the files within the folder, are now selected for backup.

8. Click **Next**. The Backup Wizard dialog box opens, prompting you to back up all selected files or changed files. By default, the "Backup all selected files" option is selected.

9. Click **Next** to back up all selected files. (That is, the files you selected in Step 7.)

10. The Backup Wizard now prompts you for a destination disk drive. In the "Where to back up" text box, enter the drive letter of the floppy drive and the filename **TestBackup**. For example, enter **A:\TestBackup**, and click **Next**. The Backup Wizard dialog box now allows you to verify the backup settings and also to select file compression in order to save disk space. Both options are selected by default.

11. Click **Next** to verify the backup settings and to compress the data into a single file. The Backup Wizard dialog box now prompts you to enter a backup job name.

12. In the Type a name for this backup job text box, enter **Test Backup**. In order to begin the backup, click **Start**. The backup process begins. The "Backup Progress - Test Backup" dialog box displays the progress and duration of the backup, as shown in Figure 14-2. Once complete, the Microsoft Backup dialog box indicates that the operation is complete.

14

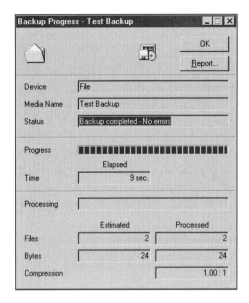

Figure 14-2 Backup Progress dialog box

13. Click **OK**. The Microsoft Backup dialog box closes, and you return to the Backup Progress – Test Backup dialog box.

14. Record the status of the backup job and whether there were any errors.

_____

15. Click **OK** to return to the **Microsoft Backup** dialog box. Now you are ready to practice restoring the backup, as described in the following steps.

16. In order to test the restore process, you will delete the file called **test2.txt**, which you created in Step 2. In a separate window, delete this file. Now you can try restoring this file, from the backup you created earlier.

17. Return to the Microsoft Backup dialog box and click **Restore**. The Microsoft Backup dialog box displays the restore options.

18. In the Restore from text box, enter the drive letter of the floppy drive and the file name **TestBackup**. For example, enter **A:\TestBackup**. (In other words, enter the same drive letter and filename you used in Step 10, earlier in this project.) Then click **Refresh**. The Microsoft Backup dialog box prompts you to refresh the current view.

19. Click **Yes**. The Select Backup Sets dialog box opens, containing the name of the backup set you created earlier in this project.

20. You want to restore the selected backup, so click **OK**. The "What to restore" pane on the left side displays the drive C.

21. Double-click the **C:** drive. The Data folder is displayed.

22. Double-click the **DATA** folder. A list of files is displayed in the right pane.

23. Click the check box next to the file named **test2.txt** in order to restore this file. A check is displayed next to the filename.

24. Click **Start**. The Media Required dialog box opens, with a list of required media. The entry "Test Backup" is the job name you entered in Step 12.

25. Click **OK**. The Restore Progress dialog box opens, indicating the progress and duration of the restore process. Record the restore status and whether there were any errors. _____
When the operation is complete, the Microsoft Backup dialog box opens. You have now successfully restored the file named test2.txt to the original directory location.

26. Click **OK** to return to the Restore Progress dialog box.

27. Click **OK** to return to the Microsoft Backup dialog box.

28. Close Microsoft Backup.

29. Open Windows Explorer and look in the folder named Data. Do you see the file named test2.txt now? _____

Review Questions

1. Explain the importance of performing a backup.

_____

_____

_____

2. Why do some companies store backups at an offsite location?

_____

_____

_____

3. Define the term disaster recovery. _____

_____

_____

4. Which of the following methods will back up only data that has been changed since the last backup?

   a. full

   b. incremental

   c. differential

   d. copy

14

5. What is the purpose of a backup rotation scheme?

_____

_____

_____

6. Which backup method will back up data regardless of whether or not the data has been changed.

   a. full

   b. incremental

   c. differential

   d. copy

7. Identify at least three key issues concerning a backup strategy.

_____

_____

_____

CHAPTER FIFTEEN

NETWORK SECURITY

Labs included in this chapter

➤ Lab 15.1 Auditing

➤ Lab 15.2 Security Risks

➤ Lab 15.3 Implementing Password Restrictions in Novell NetWare

➤ Lab 15.4 Implementing Network Address Restrictions in a Novell NetWare LAN

➤ Lab 15.5 Implementing Time of Day Restrictions in Novell NetWare

LAB 15.1 AUDITING

Objectives

The goal of this lab is to help you understand how to audit a network. After completing this lab, you will be able to:

➤ Enable auditing in Windows NT

➤ Review information on audited events

Materials Required

This lab will require the following:

➤ A Windows NT Server 4.0 computer

➤ A user account named Administrator

ACTIVITY

1. Boot the Windows NT computer. Now you can enable auditing for Windows NT; it is not enabled by default because it uses both CPU and hard disk resources.

2. In order to enable auditing in Windows NT, click **Start**, point to **Programs**, point to **Administrative Tools (Common)**, and click **User Manager for Domains**. The User Manager for Domains window opens.

3. Click **Policies**, and then click **Audit**. The Audit Policy dialog box opens.

4. Notice that the Do Not Audit option is selected by default.

5. Click the **Audit These Events** option button. You now have a choice of auditing the success or failure of seven different events.

6. Select the Success and Failure boxes for all events, as shown in Figure 15-1.

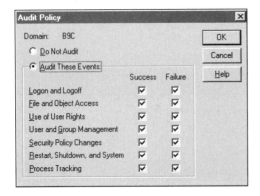

Figure 15-1 Audit Policy dialog box

7. Click **OK**. You return to the User Manager for Domains window. Auditing is now enabled.

8. Close the User Manager for Domains window. Now you will generate a logon event and logoff event.

9. Attempt to log on with the username Administrator and an incorrect password. Do this two times. Record the message you receive as a result of the incorrect password. _____
Because you enabled auditing, a record of this failure was written to a log file. In the following steps, you will display the log file in Event Viewer.

10. Log on as Administrator, using the correct password.

11. Click **Start**, point to **Programs**, point to **Administrative Tools (Common)**, and click **Event Viewer**. The Event Viewer window opens.

In order to see a record of the failed logon attempts, click **Log** on the menu bar, then click **Security**. The Security Log opens.

12. Scroll until you see a padlock icon, and then click that row. Your Security Log should look similar to the one in Figure 15-2.

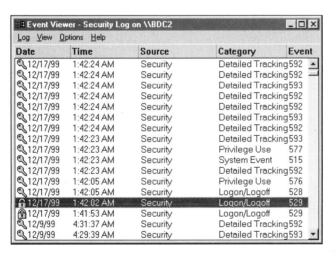

Figure 15-2 Security Log in Event Viewer

13. Double-click on the lock icon. The **Event Detail** dialog box opens, displaying specific information about the event.

14. Review the reason for failure and record it. _____

15. Close Event Viewer.

Review Questions

1. Auditing does not consume any CPU time.
   T _____ F _____

2. Explain the purpose of auditing. _____
   _____
   _____

3. Define the term authentication. _____
   _____
   _____

4. To what does the term root generally refer? _____
   _____
   _____

5. Discuss the difference between a hacker and a cracker.
   _____
   _____
   _____

Lab 15.2 Security Risks

Objective

The intent of this lab is to help you learn about network security risks. After completing this lab, you will be able to:

➤ Identify security risks

Materials Required

In this lab, you will need the following:

➤ Pencil and paper

Activity

1. Identify and discuss four security risks associated with people.
   _____
   _____
   _____
   _____

2. Identify and discuss four security risks associated with hardware and network design. _____

_____
_____
_____
_____

3. Identify and discuss four security risks associated with protocols and software.

_____
_____
_____
_____

4. Identify and discuss four security risks associated with access to the Internet. _____

_____
_____
_____
_____

Review Questions

1. Define the term social engineering. _____

_____
_____

2. The fact that UPD requires no authentication is a risk associated with hardware.
   T _____ F _____

3. The fact that wireless transmissions can be intercepted is a risk associated with protocols.
   T _____ F _____

4. Define the term IP spoofing. _____

_____
_____

5. Define the term flashing. _____

_____
_____

6. A modem allowing access to a company's network is a risk associated with people.
   T _____ F _____

7. Define the term firewall. _____

_____
_____

15

LAB 15.3 IMPLEMENTING PASSWORD RESTRICTIONS IN NOVELL NETWARE

Objective

The intent of this lab is to help you understand how to implement password restrictions in a Novell NetWare network operating system. After completing this lab, you will be able to:

➤ Implement password restrictions on a user account

Materials Required

In this lab, you will need the following:

➤ A Novell NetWare 5.0 Server computer

➤ A Windows 95/98 computer with the Novell Client software installed

➤ A functioning network connection between the two computers

➤ Completion of Lab 9.4

ACTIVITY

1. Log in to the Novell NetWare 5.0 Server as Admin from the Windows 95/98 client computer.

2. Start NetWare Administrator, following Steps 1 through 7 in Lab 9.4. (Lab 9.4 refers to the program as Nwadmn32. This is the executable program that starts NetWare Administrator.)

3. Using Lab 9.4 as a guide, create a user named TODD in the SALES container. A user object icon will appear, with the name TODD adjacent to it.

4. Double-click the icon representing the user. The properties page for the user object, named TODD, opens. Various buttons on the right side of the screen allow you to perform activities for this user object. One button is named Password Restrictions; you can use this button for settings such as requiring a password, setting minimum password length, and allowing the user to change passwords.

5. Click **Password Restrictions**. You see the Password Restrictions property page for the selected user object.

6. In order to allow the user to change passwords, make sure the "**Allow user to change password**" check box is selected.

7. In order to require a password for this user, check **Require a password**. The Minimum password length text box is enabled and displays a default value of 5. Leave the default value at 5.

8. In order to force the user to change passwords periodically, check **Force Periodic password changes**. The Days between forced changes text box is enabled and automatically set to 40 days. This is the minimum number of days that a password will be valid before the user is forced to change it. Leave the default value at 40. Also, the setting in the Date password expires box changes to the current date and time by default. This will force the password to expire immediately, thus forcing the user to change his or her password. This is useful when you want to assign a temporary password for a new user account and then force the user to select a new password upon logging in for the first time. Leave the default values.

9. In order to require a unique password for a user, check **Require unique passwords**. This prevents the user from re-using old passwords as new passwords in the future.

10. In order to limit the number of grace logins, check **Limit grace logins**. This specifies the number of times that the user can log in incorrectly before the account is disabled. Once checked, the Grace logins allowed and the Remaining grace logins settings are set to **6** by default. Your properties page should now look similar to Figure 15-3. Click **OK**.

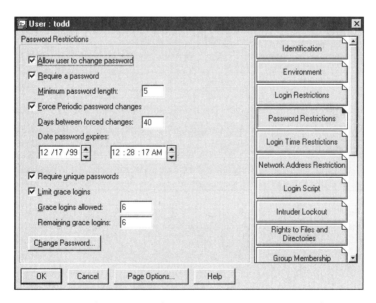

Figure 15-3 The Password Restrictions property page for a user object named TODD

11. Now you are ready to test some of these password restriction settings for the user named TODD. Log out as the Admin user.

12. Log in as the user named TODD. A message box appears indicating that you have five grace log-ins and asking if you want to change the password. Click **No**.

13 Start NetWare Administrator.

14. Double-click the icon for the user named TODD. The Property pages opens. Click **Password Restrictions** and then click **Change Password** at the bottom of the page. In order to verify the minimum password length test, attempt to create a password only three characters in length. Can you?

_____

If not, what message displayed? _____

15. Create a password eight characters in length. Can you?

_____

16. In order to verify password uniqueness, attempt to change the password again. This time, use the same password you entered in Step 13. Can you?

_____

If not, what message displayed? _____

17. Log out as the user named TODD.

Review Questions

1. Define the purpose of forcing a unique password on a user.

_____

_____

_____

2. A user's password is displayed on the screen when he or she enters it in.
   T _____ F _____

3. Define the term encryption. _____

_____

_____

4. Regardless of the network operating system, you can implement a basic security mechanism to restrict usage on the network.
   T _____ F _____

5. Define the term SSL. _____

_____

_____

LAB 15.4 IMPLEMENTING NETWORK ADDRESS RESTRICTIONS IN A NOVELL NETWARE LAN

Objectives

The intent of this lab is to help you understand how to implement network address restrictions in Novell NetWare. After completing this lab, you will be able to:

➤ Determine a node's MAC address in Novell NetWare

➤ Set network address restrictions in Novell NetWare

Materials Required

In this lab, you will need the following:

➤ A Novell NetWare 5.0 Server computer

➤ Two Windows 95/98 computers with the Novell Client software installed

➤ A functioning network connection among all three computers

➤ Completion of Lab 15.3

ACTIVITY

1. Log in to the Novell NetWare 5.0 Server as Admin from the Windows 95/98 client computer. The first workstation you use for logging in will be named "Workstation one" for purposes of this lab. The other workstation computer will be named "Workstation two."

2. Start NetWare Administrator as described in Steps 1 through 7 in Lab 9.4.

3. Double-click the user named TODD.

4. Setting network address restrictions allows you to limit the workstations from which a user can login. A user can then only use a specific workstation and is prevented by the network from logging into another computer. In order to set network address restrictions, you first need the MAC address of the computer you want the user to be able to log in to. In order to do this, you must run a command at the MS-DOS prompt. Click **Start**, point to **Programs**, and click **MS-DOS prompt**. The MS-DOS prompt dialog box opens.

5. At the prompt, type **nlist user /a** and press **Enter**. This command displays the users that are logged in, their network addresses, and their node addresses, as shown in Figure 15-4. The Network address is created during the installation of the Novell Server; it is similar to the network portion of an IP address, as discussed in Chapter 11. The node address is the actual MAC address.

15

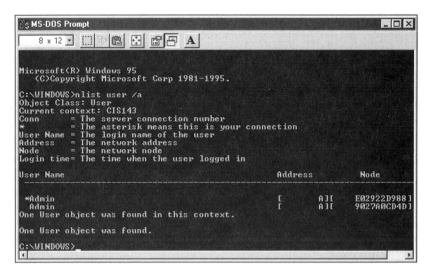

Figure 15-4 Output of the NLIST USER /A command

6. The asterisk indicates the current login session from your workstation. In Figure 15-4, this is the first entry (✶Admin). Record the network address for the entry with an asterisk next to it. _____
Remember, this should be "Workstation one."

7. Record the node address for the same entry. (The one with an asterisk next to it.) _____

8. Close the MS-DOS Prompt window.

9. On the right-hand side, click **Network Address Restrictions**. The Network Address Restrictions Property page opens. By default, there are no entries in the Network address restrictions box, meaning that the user can log in from any workstation. If there were an entry, the user could only log in from that specific workstation.

10. Notice the Network protocol section near the bottom of the screen. There are six protocols listed, with the IPX/SPX protocol selected by default. You restrict a user from using a certain computer first by selecting a protocol. Once you have selected the protocol to restrict, another dialog box appears that allows you to enter the values for the specific address of the computer you want to restrict; the type of values you enter depend upon the selected protocol.

11. Record the protocols listed for network address restriction.

12. With the IPX/SPX protocol selected by default, click **Add** in order to create a network address restriction. The IPX/SPX dialog box opens with two text boxes: Network number and Node address. Once you select a protocol to restrict, you must then specify the computer address information.

13. In the Network number text box, enter the number recorded in Step 6.

14. In the Node address text box, enter the number recorded in Step 7 and click **OK**. The Network Address Restrictions Property page returns with the network address restriction entry, similar to Figure 15-5.

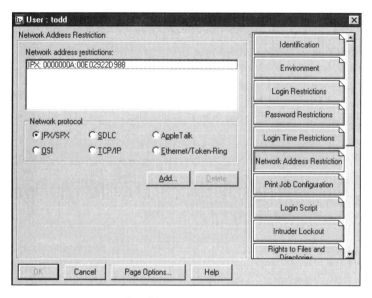

Figure 15-5 Network Address Restriction properties page

15. Close NetWare Administrator.

16. Log in as the user named TODD from "Workstation one." Can you successfully log in? _____

17. Log out as the user named TODD.

18. Log in as the user named TODD from "Workstation two." Can you successfully log in? _____
If not, what message displayed? _____

19. Log out as the user TODD.

15

Review Questions

1. Explain the purpose of network address restrictions.

   _____

   _____

   _____

2. In Novell NetWare, the node address is the MAC address of the NIC in the workstation.

   T _____ F _____

3. You can restrict an address for a computer using the TCP/IP protocol.

   T _____ F _____

4. You can restrict a network address for a user within the AppleTalk protocol.

   T _____ F _____

5. Can a hacker who has a username and password log in to any computer successfully? _____

   Explain your answer. _____

   _____

LAB 15.5 IMPLEMENTING TIME OF DAY RESTRICTIONS IN NOVELL NETWARE

Objective

The intent of this lab is to help you understand how to implement time of day restrictions in Novell NetWare. After completing this lab, you will be able to:

➤ Restrict when a user can login in to Novell NetWare

Materials Required

In this lab, you will need the following:

➤ A Novell NetWare 5.0 Server computer

➤ A Windows 95/98 computer with the Novell Client software installed

➤ A functioning network connection between the two computers

➤ Completion of Lab 9.4

ACTIVITY

1. Log in to the Novell NetWare 5.0 Server as Admin from the Windows 95/98 client computer.

2. Open NetWare Administrator as described in Steps 1 through 7 in Lab 9.4.

3. Double-click on the user object named TODD. The Property page for this user opens.

4. Click **Login Time Restrictions**. The Login Time Restrictions dialog box for the user opens, displaying rows for days and columns for time of day. By default, a user can log in on any day at any time.

5. In order to restrict a user from logging in on a certain day during a certain time, you highlight that period of time. For example, to prevent a user from logging in from 8 A.M. to 10 A.M. on Monday, you would click 8 A.M. on Monday and drag to 10 A.M. The user could then log in during any other day or time, except between 8 and 10 A.M. on Mondays. In this case, you will prevent the user from logging in any time on Friday. Use the mouse to shade the entire row for Friday, as shown in Figure 15-6.

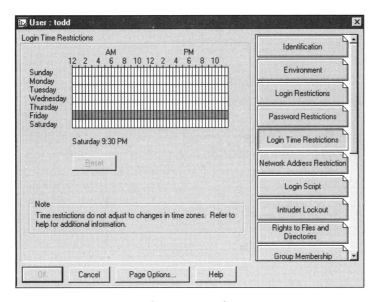

Figure 15-6   Restricting logins on Friday

6. Change the settings to allow the user to login anytime except in the next 30 minutes.

7. Click **OK**. The main property page for the user appears.

8. Close NetWare Administrator.

9. Immediately attempt to log in as the user named TODD. Can you?

_____

10. Wait for the 30 minutes to expire and then try to log in again. Can you?

_____

11. Log out of the computer as the user TODD.

Review Questions

1. Explain the purpose of restricting logins based on the time of day.

   _____

   _____

   _____

2. Specifying valid hours for logins will decrease network security.

   T _____ F _____

3. You work for a company that has three shifts of workers. You need to restrict usage based on time of day. Explain how you would do this.

   _____

   _____

   _____

4. You can combine time of day restrictions and network address restrictions for a user.

   T _____ F _____

5. Give three tips for making and keeping passwords secure.

   _____

   _____

   _____

   _____

   _____

   _____

   _____

MANAGING NETWORK DESIGN AND IMPLEMENTATION

Labs included in this chapter

➤ Lab 16.1 Planning a Network Installation

➤ Lab 16.2 Creating a PERT Chart

➤ Lab 16.3 Observing a Network Upgrade

LAB 16.1 PLANNING A NETWORK INSTALLATION

Objective

The goal of this lab is to help you understand how to plan a network installation. After completing this lab, you will be able to:

➤ Plan a network installation

Materials Required

This lab will require the following:

➤ Pencil and paper

ACTIVITY

1. Review the following scenario: You have been hired by the network manager at Todd Enterprises to install a new network. You have five network administrators at your disposal. Currently, the company runs a mainframe computer. 50 users require access to the Finance and Production applications. A software vendor has been hired to convert the application and data to a PC-based system. It's your job to plan the installation of the network. This includes the following tasks:

   a. Order PCs, cables, network cards, hubs, and network operating systems.

   b. Create a task list of activities. For example, installing the network operating system on each PC would be one task. Creating the necessary cable would be another task.

   c. Estimate each task's duration.

   d. Set precedence levels for each task. For example, you must order the hardware before you can install it.

   e. Assign tasks to each of the five network administrators.

2. To start planning the installation, complete the following task worksheet. The first task has been completed for you to give you an idea of what you need to do. Make up your own names for the five network administrators.

Project Worksheet

Number	Task Description	Precedence	Length	Person Assigned
1	Order PCs	NA	1 day	Your name goes here.

Review Questions

1. Define the term project plan. _____
   _____
   _____

2. Explain why it is important to identify task dependencies and
   predecessor tasks. _____
   _____
   _____

3. Discuss some of the types of project participants. _____
   _____
   _____

4. Explain the purpose of milestones. _____
   _____
   _____

5. Define the purpose of a feasibility study. _____
   _____
   _____

LAB 16.2 CREATING A PERT CHART

Objective

The intent of this lab is to teach you how to create a PERT chart, using
Microsoft Project 98. After completing this lab, you will be able to:

➤ Create a PERT chart, using Microsoft Project 98.

Materials Required

In this lab, you will need the following:

➤ A Windows 95/98 computer with Microsoft Project installed

16

ACTIVITY

1. In this lab, you will use Microsoft Project to create a PERT (Program
   Evaluation and Review Technique) chart. You will fill in task activities, the
   length of each task, and task precedence numbers for a network project.

The PERT chart will provide you with a graphical diagram of a project. Review the following task list:

Number	Task Description	Precedence	Duration
1	Order hardware	None	1 day
2	Order software	None	1 day
3	Install hardware	1	1 day
4	Load protocol	2	1 day
5	Access LAN	3 and 4	1 day

2. To open Microsoft Project, click **Start**, point to **Programs**, and then click **Microsoft Project**. (You might find Microsoft Project located elsewhere on your Start menu.) The Microsoft Project window along with a Welcome! dialog box opens.

3. Close the Welcome! dialog box if necessary.

4. On the left-hand side of the window, look for a column labeled Task Name. You can enter task information in this text box. On the right-hand side of the window, look for a chart that marks tasks on the calendar with boxes; this part of the window also shows precedence information. Figure 16-1 shows the window after task information has already been entered. You will enter the same information in the following steps.

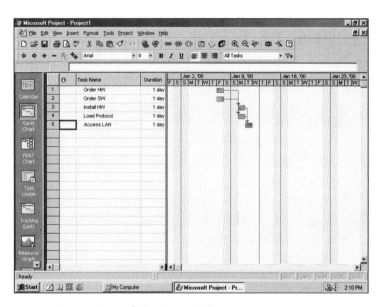

Figure 16-1 Microsoft Project window

5. In the Task Name column, enter the tasks and their duration, as given in Step 1.

6. In order to set the task dependencies for Task 3, right-click **Install Hardware** (Task number 3), and click **Task Information**. The Task Information dialog box opens with several tabs. You will make the "Order Hardware" task a predecessor to the "Install Hardware" task.

7. Click the **Predecessors** tab.

8. In the Task Name box, click **Order Hardware**. The Order Hardware task appears in the list of predecessors.

9. Click **OK**. The Precedence information on the right-hand side of the screen changes to reflect the new dependency. An arrow points from the "Order Hardware" task to the "Install Hardware" task, indicating that the latter is dependent on the former.

10. Repeat Steps 6 through 9 for the remaining tasks with predecessors.

11. Click **PERT chart** on the left-hand side of the window. A PERT chart appears, showing the task names, duration, and predecessors.

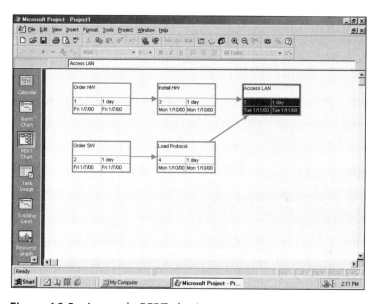

Figure 16-2   A sample PERT chart

12. Save the PERT chart.

13. Close Microsoft Project.

Review Questions

1. Define the term precedent. _____
_____
_____
_____

2. Define the term needs assessment. _____
_____
_____
_____

3. What is the purpose of a pilot network? _____
_____
_____
_____

4. Define the term contingency planning. _____
_____
_____
_____

LAB 16.3 OBSERVING A NETWORK UPGRADE

Objective

The goal of this lab is to have you observe a network upgrade. After completing this lab, you will be able to:

➤ Explain how a network upgrade is performed

Materials Required

This lab will require the following:

➤ Pencil and paper

➤ A person willing to allow you to observe a network upgrade

ACTIVITY

1. Visit the site performing a network upgrade.

2. Record the type of network operating systems used at the site.

_____
_____
_____

3. Record the protocols used at the site. _____

_____

_____

4. Record the type of topology used at the site. _____

_____

_____

5. Record any changes occurring at the site. For example, the upgrade might involve replacing Category 3 cable with Category 5 cable. Another change might involve altering the IP addressing scheme. _____

_____

_____

_____

6. Record the time required for the network upgrade. _____

_____

Review Questions

1. Define the term process management. _____

_____

_____

2. Give several reasons for having good communication methods during a network upgrade. _____

_____

_____

_____

3. Explain the importance of funding in performing a network upgrade.

_____

_____

_____

4. Explain why it is important to test the network after an upgrade.

_____

16

_____

_____

5. Explain why it is important to document any changes or problems that occur during a network upgrade. _____

_____

_____

_____